J291.9 ZEINERT
Zeinert, Karen
Cults

RIO GRANDE VALLEY
LIBRARY SYSTEM SV

Cults

Karen Zeinert

—Issues in Focus—

Enslow Publishers, Inc.

44 Fadem Road   PO Box 38
Box 699   Aldershot
Springfield, NJ 07081   Hants GU12 6BP
USA   UK

RIO GRANDE VALLEY
LIBRARY SYSTEM   SV

Copyright © 1997 by Karen Zeinert

All rights reserved.

No part of this book may be reproduced by any means
without the written permission of the publisher.

Library of Congress Cataloging-in-Publication Data

Zeinert, Karen.
   Cults / Karen Zeinert.
      p. cm. — (Issues in focus)
   Includes bibliographical references and index.
   Summary: Describes the various types of cults including their history,
characteristics, and danger to American society.
   ISBN 0-89490-900-2
   1. Cults—United States—Juvenile literature. 2. Sects—United States—
Juvenile literature. 3. United States—Religion—Juvenile literature. [1. Cults.]
I. Title. II. Series: Issues in focus (Hillside, N.J.)
BL2525.Z45   1997
291.9—dc21   96-40886
                                                       CIP
                                                       AC

Printed in the United States of America

10 9 8 7 6 5 4 3 2 1

Illustration Credits: Courtesy of AP/Wide World Photos, pp. 50, 68, 85;
Courtesy of the Dover Pictorial Archives, pp. 16, 23, 29, 42, 44, 54, 57,
90, 92, 95, 100; Courtesy of the *Fort Worth Star-Telegram*/Jerry Hoefer,
photographer, p. 9; Courtesy, National Archives, p. 64; Courtesy of *The
Plains Dealer*, Cleveland, Ohio, p. 27; Courtesy of John A. Zeinert, pp.
77, 121.

Cover Illustration: Courtesy of John A. Zeinert.

Contents

1

Making Headlines

On April 19, 1993, television screens all over the United States erupted with images of flames engulfing a group of buildings near Waco, Texas. Americans watched in horror as the flames soared high in the sky, fed by fuel that had been stored inside the compound. In minutes, the buildings were in ashes, and the community of some ninety people who lived in them had been reduced to charred skeletons.

This grim drama was the culmination of events that had begun long before April 19. The people inside the compound called themselves Branch Davidians, and their leader was David Koresh. He was the self-proclaimed messiah of their unusual religious group, a Christian cult. Koresh had long believed that the end of the world was near. Once he assumed leadership in 1988, he began to spend most of his time reading the Bible and instructing 130 followers about what would happen during the human race's last days. Koresh was especially concerned about a violent battle that he believed would take place between good and evil forces at a spot the Bible called Armageddon. According to Koresh's interpretation of the Bible, Armageddon was located near Waco.

It was Koresh's belief in this approaching showdown that eventually got the Branch Davidians into trouble with the law. To prepare for the battle, Koresh had begun to stockpile weapons. By the end of 1992, he had an impressive supply that included hundreds of guns, a grenade launcher, and eight thousand rounds of ammunition. Purchasing weapons is not against United States law, even when bought in large quantities, but turning them into weapons of war, such as machine guns, is illegal. When authorities in the United States Bureau of Alcohol, Tobacco and Firearms (ATF) were informed by a delivery man that the Davidians were receiving many weapons as well as parts that would enable the Davidians to make machine guns, they were concerned. They worried about what the cult members would do with the guns, fearing that Koresh might sell some to make money, thereby spreading dangerous weapons throughout the country. As a result, the ATF began to investigate the cult's activities.

By mid-February 1993, ATF agents believed that they had enough proof to bring Koresh in for questioning. On February 28, they went to the compound to arrest him. A shoot-out took place—both sides claimed that the other shot first—and when the bullets stopped flying, four ATF agents and six Davidians were dead. In addition, sixteen agents were wounded, as were a number of Davidians, including Koresh himself.

To avoid further bloodshed, ATF agents, now joined by members of the Federal Bureau of Investigation (FBI), decided to lay siege to the compound. But because the Davidians had large stores of food on hand and their own source of water, frustrated agents estimated that the Davidians could hold out for at least two years.

To speed up a surrender, federal agents began to blast the compound with noise (including tapes containing the screams of dying animals) night and day to make the Davidians as uncomfortable as possible and to deprive them of sleep. This, too, failed to bring about a surrender, although thirty-five Davidians did decide to leave the compound during the first four weeks of the noisy siege.

Even though the federal agents' plan had produced some results, the siege had been going on for seven weeks and stories started to surface about child abuse in the cult. Officials decided to take drastic steps to force the Davidians to surrender. After several unsuccessful last-minute appeals to the Davidians to come out, agents assaulted the compound. Early in the morning on April 19, military tanks punched holes in the compound's walls and fired canisters of tear gas toward cult members. A few minutes later, the first flames appeared.

Far from forcing the Davidians to give in, the attack convinced them that they were witnessing the first round of the highly anticipated violent battle that would mark the beginning of the end of the world. Certain now that Satan himself was at their gate, the Davidians became more determined than ever not to surrender. To do so, they believed, would mean eternal damnation. So all but nine followers remained in the compound, burning to death with their leader. The survivors were taken into custody and questioned about the tragedy.

Uproar over Waco

A heated debate about the events at Waco on April 19 began almost as soon as the flames died down. Davidian supporters claimed that federal agents had deliberately set the compound ablaze. Some supporters argued that the Davidians had been targeted for persecution by the government because of their religious beliefs. Others insisted that the Davidians had been massacred because they had stockpiled weapons. All seethed with rage when they described how the government had spied on the compound, and they sneered with disgust when they talked about an informant the agents had placed inside.

Supporters, fearing that similar fates might befall others who shared Koresh's beliefs, demanded an investigation. "There were law-abiding, God-fearing people in there," said Koresh's mother, Bonnie Haldeman. "They didn't hurt anybody."[1] Why, she wanted to know, had they been attacked and their compound burned?

The official government story was that the Davidians themselves were responsible for the tragedy. Agents insisted that the fires had been started inside the compound. Agent Byron Sage said, "I saw three fires almost simultaneously. There's no question but that it was not started by the tanks in front of [the buildings]. . . . I saw the tanks at different points from where the fires were."[2] Agents added that the whole crisis could have been

Flames raced through the Branch Davidians' compound near Waco, Texas, on April 19, 1993.

avoided if only the Davidians had surrendered. And they pointed out that they gave Koresh and his followers fifty-one days to do so.

The uproar continued for months. Antiterrorist experts in other federal departments joined in the argument, privately criticizing the ATF agents and their leaders, some of whom were eventually fired. News reporters publicly charged the ATF with incompetence. And the public wondered aloud about what really had happened in Waco.

The outcry was so great that the United States Department of Justice decided to hold an investigation later that year to determine who was responsible for the tragedy. When the investigating panel concluded that the Davidians had been responsible for the fires, relatives and supporters of the men and women who had died in the inferno accused the government of a cover-up.

Instead of accepting the panel's conclusion, supporters went to court. They filed lawsuits that sought more than $1.5 billion in compensation from the government, which they held responsible for the deaths of their loved ones.[3] Some supporters were so deeply upset over the raid and the investigation that they began to refer to the government as Satan.

Repercussions?

On the second anniversary of the attack on the Davidians, April 19, 1995, Americans were once again stunned by devastating news. A bomb had gone off in front of the Alfred P. Murrah Federal Building in Oklahoma City, Oklahoma, and the first reports indicated that at least one hundred people were dead and another hundred were missing.

One of the men arrested shortly after the bombing, Timothy McVeigh, had been very upset by the events in Waco. In fact, a former coworker, in an FBI affidavit, claimed that the bombing suspect was unusually angry at the government and the role it had played in the Branch Davidians' deaths.[4] As a result, many reporters began to wonder whether the suspect—if he was indeed guilty— had decided to punish the government by deliberately destroying one of its buildings and killing federal employees.

Suspicions, rumors, and questions abounded as federal agents and the public tried to make sense of what had happened. In short, the events at Waco just would not go away. Now Americans wondered not only about the Branch Davidians, but about all cults in general. What exactly was a cult, anyway? How many more cults, they asked, were hunkered down in compounds scattered across the United States? Were all cults alike? And most important, what dangers did they and their supporters present?

2

What Is a Cult?

The presence of cults in America is a very emotional and controversial issue, due in large part to highly publicized events like the burning of the Branch Davidian compound. As a result, no religious group wants to be thought of as a cult, and almost any definition offered is hotly contested. It is not surprising, then, that there are many definitions of "cult" in use today.

Some conservative and vocal Christian leaders insist that any religious group that is non-Christian is a cult. This includes churches that have broken away from a Christian organization to form their own group or sect because they questioned a fundamental Christian belief. According to this definition, millions of Americans would be considered cultists, including the Branch Davidians, Jehovah's Witnesses, Mormons, and Christian Scientists.

Secular opponents (people who are not ministers or members of any clergy) identify cults by their practices and lifestyles, not by their religious beliefs. Secular opponents include national organizations such as the Cult Awareness Network and the Council on Mind Abuse. Most members of these organizations, generally called anticultists, define cults as groups that are led by an all-powerful leader or leaders who claim to have special abilities or powers. Members also claim that cult leaders demand total loyalty, discourage rational thought, and may even insist that followers sever all ties with friends and family in order to devote their lives to the cult. The secular opponents' idea of what a cult is has become the definition most commonly accepted by the American public.

Because this definition identifies a lifestyle so different from that of the average American, one would not expect to find many cult members in the United States. However, anticultists believe that as many as five thousand cults are flourishing in America and that up to 20 million Americans have been members of these organizations in the course of the last twenty years.[1]

A third definition of cults in use today, developed by some social scientists (historians and sociologists, for example), simply identifies cults as groups of people whose beliefs or lifestyles are very different from those of their neighbors. These beliefs may be brought into a society from another country, or they may develop within the country itself. By this definition, Hinduism and Buddhism would be considered cults in the United States. Both religions, which were brought to America from Asia, vary greatly from Christianity and Judaism, currently the most popular faiths in the United States. On the other hand, Christianity would be thought of as a cult in many Asian countries, where only a few Christians live, just as it was when it began nearly two thousand years ago. Because the word "cult" has such a negative image, many social scientists refuse to use it; instead, they use the terms "new religion" or "alternative religion" when referring to groups with unusual faiths.

Social scientists believe that there are fewer than two hundred thousand cultists in the United States today. Most members belong to one of some six hundred groups, many of which, like the Branch Davidians, are very small, with less than a few hundred members each.[2]

Many groups have been identified as cults over the years by conservative Christian leaders, anticultists, and social scientists. In some cases, only one of the three considered an organization a cult; in other cases, all three labeled it as such. The Branch Davidians, for instance, would fit all three definitions. The vast majority of cult members have shared common religious beliefs; however, some members have been united by a common political goal, or even a particular fad. Because it would be very difficult to include all of these groups in a single book, only the best-known, headline-making, controversial groups are discussed here. Together, the different groups give a broad overview of the complex issue of cults, and the selection includes doomsday groups, Spiritualists, snake handlers, Eastern religious groups, Christian revivalists, and Satanists—a diverse mix, to say the least.

Who Joins a Cult?

Historically, people everywhere have developed religious beliefs. Many people seek out a God or gods in whom to believe to give meaning and purpose to their lives as well as to help them endure life's trials and tribulations. Faith also enables followers to face death with confidence if their religion includes a belief in heaven or an afterlife. In fact, many religious groups have developed a specific code of behavior that will enable followers to gain eternal life. Sometimes this code clashes with the law, but true believers follow it anyway because, if they do not, they think that they will be doomed to spend eternity in hell, a place that, although described differently by different religions, has never been pictured as pleasant.

Throughout the ages, people have tended to turn to religion, especially new religions, during times of great social, political, or economic upheaval. Overwhelmed by epidemics, devastating wars, financial ruin, or other calamities, men and women may seek new gods simply because the old ones failed to protect them.

In addition, individuals may look for a faith or a different religion to follow during times of serious personal problems. These problems may be caused by the death of a loved one or a heart-wrenching end to a romantic relationship or the failure to achieve an especially important goal. Young adults who are trying to find themselves and to establish their goals in life may also seek out different religious groups during these sometimes difficult years. Some of these groups will be cults.

In general, no matter what definition is used, cult members share a number of similar characteristics. The majority are idealistic, single, male, white, middle-class, and young, many being eighteen to twenty-five years old. Most have been members of the Christian or Jewish communities, and they have attended services regularly.

15

Many people today picture hell as a site of eternal flames and agony like John Milton described more than three hundred years ago in his famous book *Paradise Lost*.

Approximately 60 percent of cult members have attended college, although only 20 percent have received a degree.[3]

Even though members are often portrayed as mentally ill because their lifestyles and beliefs are unusual, they do not, as a group, experience many more psychological problems than the public at large. Some mental health experts have estimated that approximately 75 percent of all cult members are basically mentally healthy individuals. By comparison, 33 percent of all adults have had emotional problems at one time or another, and at any given time 10 percent of the general population suffers from mental illness. In some large urban areas the incidence of serious emotional problems among the general public may run as high as 23 percent.[4]

David Wallace, a medical student who joined a cult called the Divine Light Mission after his grades hit an all-time low, described typical cult membership:

> The people I ended up [being] with were very intelligent and very idealistic people. But there were some real zonkers in the group, at least in New York. . . . I'd say, generally though, most people I knew seemed pretty normal and had a lot of potential. They were artists and people who dropped out of their first and second year of college. They were the most intelligent group, who maybe were not so career minded but definitely had heads on their shoulders.[5]

The Branch Davidians, like David Wallace's group, also contained a number of highly educated people. For example, one of David Koresh's most trusted assistants, Steve Schneider, had been an instructor in religious studies at the University of Hawaii. Another follower, Wayne

Martin, was a graduate of Harvard Law School and a law librarian at the University of North Carolina before he moved to the compound in Waco, Texas.

Who Leads Cults?

Just as cult members share similar characteristics, so do cult leaders, especially those who have made headlines. In general, many of these leaders have had unusual lives that were filled with traumatic experiences and uncommon visions. Few have been able to fit into ordinary society even though they may be highly intelligent, extremely charming (when they want to be), and very ambitious people. In addition, they are charismatic—that is, they have an extraordinary ability to persuade people to believe in them and their cause.

David Koresh certainly fit this pattern. Koresh, who was born in 1959 in Texas, had few friends as a child, and he was often a victim of bullies, who repeatedly assaulted him. Even though he was very bright, he had great difficulty learning to read because he suffered from dyslexia. As a result of his learning disability he was assigned to special education classes. Frustrated and unhappy, Koresh dropped out of school in the ninth grade. He held a number of low-paying jobs, working at gas stations and garages for several years, while he practiced playing his guitar, hoping someday to become a successful entertainer.

Like many other cult leaders, Koresh's interest in religion began early. As a small boy, he often attended church with his grandmother, a Seventh-Day Adventist. When he was about twenty years old, Koresh heard a leader of the Branch Davidians named Lois Roden preach. Shortly afterward, he became involved in the Davidian group. When he tried to take control in 1984 and failed to do so, Koresh was forced to leave the compound. He spent the next three years wandering throughout the world, looking for followers.

By 1987, Koresh, claiming to have experienced a religious awakening that gave him great insight, had convinced nine families to believe in him. He then returned to Waco with his supporters, where he was able to persuade others that he was special. Within a year he had become the Davidians' leader.

Cults Galore

Although cults make headlines in America, they are not new, nor are they limited to the United States. Information about cults has appeared in many accounts of some of the oldest and best known civilizations, including those of the Romans and the Egyptians.

More recently, cults in Switzerland and France have grabbed the public's attention. In October 1994, Swiss police found the grisly remains of forty-eight cult members who belonged to the Order of the Solar Temple. In December 1995, sixteen bodies of members belonging to the same cult were found in France. At first, it appeared that cult members in both cases had participated in a murder-suicide pact. Later, police suspected that the cultists had been murdered, possibly by rival cult members.

Another cult received international attention when it placed poisonous gas in the subway system in Tokyo,

Japan. The attackers had intended to strike a blow at the government, which opposed the cult, by attempting to kill the 6 million people who use Tokyo's subway system daily. However, the poison did not work as planned. Even so, this botched attempt injured almost five thousand people and killed twelve.

Although other nations have had their share of cults, few countries have had the sheer number found in America. This large number is due to at least three factors. First, many different faiths were brought to North America by immigrants who arrived from all over the world. Native Americans were the first to introduce religious beliefs in what is now the United States, when they arrived from Asia more than thirty thousand years ago. In the 1600s, the first colonists from Europe—Puritans, Catholics, Quakers, Moravians, Huguenots, Anabaptists, and Lutherans—began to arrive. Before long, Africans who had been enslaved became unwilling immigrants, and they brought another set of religious beliefs with them. As other immigrants entered over the years, more faiths, such as Buddhism and Islam, began to appear. When groups interacted and exchanged ideas, new beliefs developed, some of which led to the formation of cults.

The second factor that made it possible for many cults to develop is the First Amendment to the United States Constitution. It forbids the government from interfering with citizens' religious beliefs, stating that "Congress shall make no law respecting an establishment of religion, or prohibiting the free exercise thereof." This gives Americans almost unlimited opportunity to worship as they please, no matter how strange their beliefs may appear to others.

The third factor that encouraged the growth of cults was the phenomenon of religious revivals that from time to time swept across America, most notably in the early 1800s and the mid-1900s. During the first revival, preachers traveled throughout the country, pitching tents here and there for day-long services that attracted thousands of participants. Twentieth-century speakers used radio and television to reach millions of people. Scathing sermons that vividly described conditions in hell caused Americans to examine their old beliefs more closely, and some decided to abandon them.

In the early 1800s, for example, many people left their churches and formed or joined one of several cults that were springing up then, especially in New England, which was a hotbed of new and varied religious beliefs. William Ellery Channing shocked fellow Congregationalists when he questioned the belief that God and Christ were part of a trinity, and he was told to leave the church. Shortly afterward, he started the Unitarian Church. At about the same time, Isaac Bullard led a small band throughout New England seeking others who regarded the dirt and sweat derived from hard work as divine. Bullard had not bathed for seven years, and he expected his followers to do likewise.

Opposition to Cults

Ironically, even though there were many factors that encouraged cults to form from the earliest colonial days to the present, cults have encountered great opposition in America. Although many people with many different religious beliefs settled the colonies, at first each group tended to occupy its own area, far away from the others. The exception to this pattern was the Religious Society of Friends, commonly known as Quakers. Until William Penn obtained a charter in 1681 to start a colony for Quakers in what is now Pennsylvania, where religious freedom for all was practiced, most Quakers settled anywhere they could purchase land. By isolating themselves and refusing to accept settlers of different faiths, and driving them out if they managed to get in, religious groups in the majority in a colony assured themselves that they could maintain control. This was very important to groups that had been too weak to protect themselves from persecution in Europe and had suffered greatly as a result.

Religious persecution of minority groups in America continued for many years, and some, especially supporters of the Branch Davidians, would argue that it still exists. Over the decades, a shocking number of leaders of religious cults have been assassinated, and cult members have been harassed, assaulted, driven out of town, and, like some of their leaders, murdered. Today, many cult members argue that they have been denied their constitutional rights to worship as they please. They are, they insist, harmless groups intent only upon trying to save their souls and worship their God.

On the other hand, critics of cults scoff at the cults' claim that they are only searching for paradise; instead, they describe a very frightening situation. Some conservative Christian leaders believe that cult members are putting their souls in danger by refusing to embrace Christianity. Anticultists believe that cults can endanger followers' well-being and even their lives. These

William Penn received land in what is now Pennsylvania from the king of England in 1681. There he started a colony for Quakers, who had been persecuted in almost all other colonies.

opponents cite cases where leaders have physically and mentally abused cult members, including children. Leaders also have convinced cult members to die with them. Cults, critics argue, are dangerous organizations, and their activities ought to be opposed and even curbed.

Sometimes average citizens, enraged and upset by events like those in Waco, wonder aloud if cults should not somehow be eliminated. Legislative hearings have even been held in several states to explore the possibility of regulating cults. To date, none has resulted in anticult laws.

Neither cult members nor anticultists, religious and secular, show any sign of abandoning their cause, and both continue to gather information to make their case before the American public. So the controversy over cults continues, and it is very unlikely that it will end soon.

3

The End of the World Is Near: Apocalyptic Cults

Precisely at 6:30 P.M. on April 17, 1989, twenty men, women, and children, members of a small cult, sat down to eat their dinner in the old farmhouse near Kirtland, Ohio, where they had lived for the past two years. It would be the last meal for five of the cult's members, the Avery family—the rest of the group had decided to kill them.

When dinner was finished, Jeffrey Lundgren, the cult's leader, accompanied by Ron Luft, Greg Winship, Richard Brand, Danny Kraft, and Lundgren's eighteen-year-old son, Damon, went to the barn to check out the site where the murders would be carried out. Satisfied that everything was in place, the six men proceeded with their plan. Luft went back to the house to ask Dennis Avery to come to the barn. As soon as Avery entered the building, the men overwhelmed him, bound his feet and arms, and lowered him into a deep pit. Jeffrey Lundgren then took aim with his pistol and shot Avery twice, while

Winship ran a chain saw to cover the sound of the gunfire. Next, Dennis's wife, Cheryl, was called to the barn. When she lay dead in the pit, fifteen-year-old Trina, thirteen-year-old Becky, and six-year-old Karen were lured to the barn, one by one, and killed.

After the men had concealed the bodies, they returned to the house. They joined the women in the living room, read several passages from the Bible, and then retired for the night.

The following day, as planned, the cult members quit their jobs and left Ohio. Their vans were stuffed with food, tents, and camping gear, which they planned to use while living in a wooded area near Davis, West Virginia. It was there, now that they had sacrificed the Averys, that they expected Christ to appear.

Shortly after the Averys were murdered, Cheryl Avery's mother contacted the police. She had become alarmed when her daughter suddenly stopped phoning her. The police then began to look for the Averys, whom they assumed had left town with the rest of the cult. The officers were unable to locate Lundgren's camping area until November, more than six months after the murders. Before they could be questioned, however, the cult members pulled up their tent stakes and headed west, frightened off when they saw police nearby.

The information the police needed to find the Averys was given to them on December 31, 1989, when a cult member named Keith Johnson went to ATF officials in Kansas City, Missouri. Johnson, who had not participated in the murders, was infuriated when he found out that his wife had been seduced by Lundgren. To punish the cult leader, Johnson decided to turn him in for the murders.

The next day, digging crews began the gruesome task of finding the Averys' badly decomposed bodies.

Working on tips supplied by Johnson as well as several other cult members who agreed to help, police located and arrested Lundgren and the other murderers in less than a week after all the bodies were found. The accused were brought back to Ohio for their trials in March 1990. Each was tried separately.

The Kirtland Massacre Trials

The cult members' trials made headlines all across the United States. People were fascinated by the events because the killers' claims were so incredible. From the very beginning, Lundgren, a Mormon (a member of the Reorganized Church of Jesus Christ of Latter Day Saints) who was well versed in the Bible, insisted that he was a prophet who had found coded messages in the Bible that gave him special knowledge about the end of the world. He said that he was only doing what he had to do, offering human sacrifices to get Christ to return to usher in doomsday, after which heaven on earth would follow.

All of the others tried for murder insisted that they killed the Averys because they believed that Christ would not return without a blood sacrifice. Like Lundgren, they also believed that Armageddon would take place at a Mormon temple in Kirtland, which was then owned by the Reorganized Latter Day Saints. Lundgren and some of his followers had at one time been employed by the temple to give tours of the building. To capture this temple, cult members had gathered weapons and made detailed plans to seize and hold the site. Preparations, cult

Jeffrey Lundgren, shown in the middle, was a cult leader in Ohio.

members told unbelieving spectators in the courtroom, had included numerous military drills near the building, while townspeople slept at night.

The juries found all who were involved in the murders guilty. Lundgren's followers, including his wife, were given prison terms; Jeffrey Lundgren was sentenced to die in the electric chair.

Apocalyptic Cults

Lundgren was a leader of what is known as a doomsday or apocalyptic cult, a cult that foresees the appearance of its God, the end of the world, and the beginning of paradise on earth. Some groups with Christian roots believe that Christ will reappear before the battle takes place at Armageddon; others believe that he will return after the forces of good win. Cultists who believe that

27

Christ, or their God, will then rule for a thousand years are sometimes known as millennial cults. This term is also used to describe cults that believe doomsday will arrive at the turn of the century, in A.D. 2001, for example.

The idea of a violent end to the world has been part of traditional Christian beliefs for two thousand years, and it has been vividly described in Revelation, or the Apocalypse, the last book of the Bible. Part of the description includes four horsemen, who, like the thundering mounts they ride, brutally trample and destroy all evil men and women on the last day. Christians brought the idea of a violent end of the world to the colonies, and many cults adopted it over the years.

Jehovah's Witnesses

Few have done more to publicly promote doomsday than have the Jehovah's Witnesses. This cult, which uses a form of the Hebrew name for God, "Yahweh," as part of its title, was started in the 1870s by Charles Taze Russell, when he began to hold special Bible study classes. Russell was a former member of the Seventh-Day Adventists, a group that holds its religious services on the seventh day of the week, Saturday. Jehovah's Witnesses have periodically set dates when the conflagration would happen: 1914, 1918, 1925, and 1975. When the end failed to materialize in 1975, membership fell. The Witnesses currently have more than nine hundred thousand members in the United States and more than 4 million worldwide. A definite date for the end of the world is no longer publicized.

The Four Horsemen of the Apocalypse are shown here in a famous print made by Albrecht Dürer in 1498. The horsemen represent human hardships, specifically Conquest, War, Famine, and Death.

The American public, in general, has regarded Jehovah's Witnesses with skepticism and even hostility because of their religious beliefs. Witnesses are pacifists, and they will not fight in any war. In addition, they do not celebrate holidays or birthdays, and they will not salute the American flag, believing that to do so violates biblical passages that warn readers about bowing down before images and idols. To a Witness, saluting something is the same as bowing down before it, a sin that can result in eternal destruction. Because of these positions, sentiment against Witnesses has run fairly high during certain periods in history, especially during wartime. After America entered World War II in 1941, for example, Witnesses were threatened and driven out of cities in Mississippi, Texas, California, Arkansas, and Wyoming.[1]

Christian Identity Groups

While the Witnesses tried to predict when the world would end and prepared for it through prayer and repentance, some apocalyptic cults, like Koresh's and Lundgren's, have taken steps to defend themselves against any and all evil forces set loose on doomsday. Among the most militant of these cults are Christian Identity groups.

The Christian Identity movement consists of numerous groups that believe that people of Anglo-Saxon, Scandinavian, and Germanic ancestry are descendants of the ancient tribes of Israel. This ancestry, or "identity," according to believers, makes them God's chosen people with whom a special covenant has been made: They will inherit the earth.

Although beliefs of Christian Identity members vary from cult to cult, they share several convictions. Most members believe that all but the children of Israel are inferior people, and some cult members have strong ties to the Ku Klux Klan and the American Nazi party. In addition, many Identity members believe that America is God's chosen land for his chosen people, and they are armed and prepared to fight to make the United States an Identity homeland. The names of some of the groups reflect Identity beliefs: the Anglo-Saxon Federation of America; the Christian-Patriots Defense League; the Church of Jesus Christ Christian, Aryan Nations; Your Heritage; and The Covenant, the Sword, the Arm of the Lord.

To prepare for doomsday, Identity groups have taken several steps. Most have staked out an area that they feel they can defend, primarily in the West or Midwest. They have also armed themselves heavily, built up alliances with other Identity groups, and learned how to be self-sufficient, producing most of what they need to survive by their own hands in their homes and gardens.

But just as in David Koresh's case, accumulating a stockpile of weapons has brought these cultists into conflict with the law. A number of Identity leaders have been arrested and convicted of violating federal gun laws.

The Weavers at Ruby Ridge

One of the most publicized conflicts involving an Identity member and the government was the Randy Weaver case. Weaver, his wife, Vicki, and their five children lived on Ruby Ridge near Naples, Idaho. Randy Weaver was buying guns, and his purchases aroused interest in the ATF.

When Weaver failed to report for questioning, ATF agents began to scout his property in the wilderness,

31

looking for the easiest way to arrest him. On August 21, 1992, as the agents neared the house, shots rang out, and Weaver's fourteen-year-old son, Samuel, and Deputy United States Marshal William Degan were killed. Having failed to make an easy arrest, the agents then laid siege to Weaver's cabin. Given orders to shoot on sight, they fired at Weaver's friend, Kevin Harris, who was armed. The bullet passed through Harris and struck and killed Weaver's wife, Vicki, who was holding an infant in her arms. Shortly after, Weaver was taken into custody.

Christian Identity cults were outraged by the shoot-out, and they demanded an investigation. The first was held in 1994. When the Justice Department decided that none of the ATF agents would be charged with federal crimes for the shootings, Weaver's supporters were furious. Later, when reporters discovered that agency records had been destroyed before the hearing, supporters shouted "Cover-up!"

A second hearing was held in 1995, when Congress, deeply concerned about the actions of the ATF and the FBI in Waco, began to think anew about the agencies' actions at Ruby Ridge. A scathing report was issued, but no criminal charges were filed.

The Freemen of Montana

Other Christian Identity members ran into trouble with the law early in 1996. A group calling themselves the Freemen (because they no longer considered themselves United States citizens) was accused of threatening to kill a federal judge and issuing bogus checks worth millions of dollars. When federal agents arrived to arrest the

Freemen on March 25, 1996, the group hunkered down on a ranch near Jordan, Montana. They were heavily armed and refused to surrender. When the FBI surrounded the ranch, many Americans began to fear that another Waco was about to happen. However, a series of people, one of whom was Randy Weaver, offered to talk to the Freemen and encourage them to leave the ranch, and they were eventually successful in their efforts. On the eighty-first day of the siege, June 13, all sixteen Freemen, men and women, surrendered to authorities.

Meanwhile, other Identity groups continue to prepare for Armageddon, and federal agents, greatly alarmed by the growing number of such groups, watch them very carefully. Understandably, the agents fear more confrontations—confrontations that may not end peacefully.

The Family

Eagerly anticipating doomsday and fearing that it might not occur in the near future, some apocalyptic cults look for ways to bring it about as soon as possible. One of these cults was known as the Family. It was headed by one of the most notorious cult leaders in America, Charles Manson, who founded his group in San Francisco in 1967. He began with one follower, Mary Brunner, a librarian.

By the time Manson founded his cult at the age of thirty-two, he had spent more than half of his life in penal institutions for a variety of crimes that included theft and fraud. Despite his criminal background and his unkempt appearance, with long straight hair and untrimmed beard, he managed to find followers by convincing them that he was Christ. Although he probably never had more than thirty followers at any time, many were so devoted that they would kill for him on command.

Manson's view of paradise was different from that of most cult leaders. He believed that heaven was located in a bottomless pit, the entrance of which was a cave hidden somewhere in Death Valley, California. According to a former Family member, the cult leader had claimed:

> Every tuned-in tribe of people that's ever lived [has] escaped the destruction of [its] race by going underground, literally, and they're all living in a golden city where there's a river that runs through it of milk and honey, and a tree that bears twelve kinds of fruit, a different fruit each month . . . and you don't need to bring candles nor any flashlights down there. He says it will be all lit up because . . . the walls will glow and it won't be cold and it won't be too hot. There will be warm springs and fresh water, and people are already down there waiting for him.[2]

Manson was convinced that the entrance's location would not be made known to him until doomsday arrived, so he plotted to bring about the end. After moving the Family to Death Valley, Manson devised a plan that he called "Helter Skelter," his term for a civil war between African Americans and whites. To start the war, Manson told four of his followers, all white, to slaughter some white victims. Manson assumed that local citizens would think that African Americans had committed the crime and take action on their own. One retaliation would lead to another and another, and chaos would result.

On the night of August 9, 1969, cult members Susan Atkins, Patricia Krenwinkel, Linda Kasabian, and Charles Watson went to a house in Bel Air, a suburb of Los Angeles, and killed five people: Sharon Tate, a movie actress who lived in the house and was eight months pregnant; three house guests, Jay Sebring, Abigail Folger, and Wojiciech Frykowski; and Steven Parent, who happened to stop by the house.

The next night, some of Manson's followers went to a Los Angeles suburb, Los Feliz, and murdered two more victims: Leno LaBianca and his wife, Rosemary. As in the Tate murders, the LaBiancas were stabbed repeatedly; Leno had twenty-six wounds, including one from a kitchen fork, and his wife had been stabbed forty-one times. And, just as in the Tate murders, the killers had dipped a towel into the blood pooled around one of the victims and written "Death to Pigs," "Rise," and "Healter Skelter," misspelled, on the walls.

The riot Manson envisioned did not take place. Instead, he and the killers in the cult were eventually arrested, tried, found guilty of murder, and sentenced to prison for life. During the investigation, authorities came to believe that the Family had been responsible for at least thirty-five murders over the years.

This cult did not disband when Manson went to prison. Instead, members continued to live together near San Francisco, waiting for the day that Manson would be free.

The Family made headlines again on September 5, 1975, when cult member Lynette "Squeaky" Fromme tried to assassinate President Gerald Ford because she was upset over the way he was running the country. Ford was visiting San Francisco, and he was scheduled to make a brief public appearance in one of the city's parks as he walked to a meeting. After selecting a spot along the sidewalk earlier that day, Fromme simply waited for the president to arrive. As Ford approached her, she pulled out her gun. While she was taking aim, Secret Service men spotted her and wrestled her to the ground before she could fire. She was tried, convicted, and sentenced to life in prison.

This cult continues to frighten the public. Although the murderers are still behind bars, all but Fromme are now eligible for parole. Hearings are held every five years to decide if Family members should be freed. Each time, frightened citizens have appeared before the parole board to demand that Manson and his followers remain in prison, a request that has been honored—so far.

4

Heaven on Earth: Utopian Cults

While nineteenth-century apocalyptic cults prepared for an impending doomsday and the paradise they believed would follow, other cults sought to create heaven on earth through their own efforts while they waited for their God to arrive. These cults started exclusive, self-supporting communities. Isolated from the sinful world, just as the Puritans had been, believers hoped to lead perfect lives.

In most cases, followers were expected to share their worldly goods as well as work for the betterment of their community. Usually, members sold their belongings and gave the proceeds to the leader. Jobs were assigned by the leader or a committee. In all cases, the success of the community was most important; individual needs and wants were secondary. For instance, if more crops had to be raised, more people were told to work in the fields, and they were expected to do so even if they did not particularly like to plant corn or harvest potatoes.

Most of these communities were religious in nature, although a few were organized as social experiments in which religion did not play a factor. Because these communes sought perfection, they were sometimes called utopias, after a site first described as an ideal place to live in Sir Thomas More's book *Utopia* (1516). How these utopias fared depended greatly upon their leaders. Few were up to the enormous challenge, and the majority of the 129 communes that have been documented so far failed within twenty years. Many were started by groups in Europe, primarily in Germany, who then came to the United States seeking religious freedom. However, three cults that have received the most attention, the Shakers, the Mormons, and the People's Temple, were made up primarily of Americans.

The Shakers

One of the earliest and longest-lived utopian experiments in America was that of the Shakers. This cult was started by a poor Englishwoman, Ann Lee, who had long been suspected of being a witch. Lee arrived in the colonies in 1774, less than a year before the Revolutionary War began. According to Lee, who had many visions, Christ had come to earth again—in spirit. This spirit lived in Ann Lee.

Lee and nine followers, including her husband, purchased some land near Albany, New York, where they started the Church of Christ's Second Appearing. Lee's religious ideas appealed to many, and she quickly built an impressive following in the New England area. Because members often trembled as they anticipated visions or entered trances during religious services, her followers became known as Shakers.

When the American Revolution broke out in 1775, Lee condemned the patriots, calling them unchristian for fighting. Her verbal assaults, which increased over the years, understandably upset the patriots. By 1780, she had convinced quite a few colonists in the area that the war was a sinful undertaking. As a result, local militias had difficulty recruiting soldiers.

Militia leaders decided to silence Lee. They put her in jail for a while, hoping to teach her a lesson. However, when Lee was released, she continued to give antiwar speeches. Next, thugs assaulted her in her home, dragged her outside, threw her into a sleigh, and took her to a neighbor's house where she was forced to endure a humiliating strip search. When this failed to quiet her, local militias gave up.

The Shakers eventually established eighteen villages; most were located in New England, and most had fewer than two hundred members. Life in these communes was very simple. Excess in anything, including pride, was discouraged, and as the Shakers believed that in working well they were praising God, they made clothing, furniture, and household goods in a uniquely simple, beautiful style that was greatly admired by visitors. In fact, people still buy Shaker furniture today, especially antique collectors.

Ann Lee's belief that members should never have sexual relations caused outsiders to ridicule the Shakers. This belief also limited their number, because they did not have children of their own. Instead, Lee's followers counted on converts and the adoption of orphans to swell their ranks. To attract converts, Shaker missionaries held meetings all over New England to explain their beliefs. These meetings angered townspeople who were afraid that the Shakers might lure members away from local churches. Mobs quickly formed wherever the Shakers chose to speak, and some angry citizens drove the missionaries right out of the area. In spite of such opposition, the Shakers were able to find new followers. However, over the years, the number of converts dwindled and many of the orphans refused to remain members as adults. Today, more than two hundred years after the cult was formed, only a few elderly Shakers remain.

The Mormons

The Shakers were not alone in encountering violence for their beliefs; the Mormons also faced hostile and dangerous mobs. The Church of Jesus Christ of Latter-day Saints, more commonly called the Mormon Church, was founded by Joseph Smith in New York State in 1830. Smith claimed that seven years earlier, while praying, he was approached by an angel who told him that many of the ancient prophecies were about to be fulfilled. This angel, Moroni, appeared often to Smith. Moroni talked about his time on earth as an historian for an ancient people who had migrated from Jerusalem to the American continent. He also told Smith where he could find inscribed golden plates that would not only give details of America's ancient history but provide words of faith and wisdom as well. Smith located and translated the plates, and with the help of friends, he published the results in *The Book of Mormon*, which was named in honor of Moroni's father, Mormon. Within months, Smith had several hundred followers. This group then began a drive to raise enough funds to build a church in Kirtland, Ohio, the spot where they believed that Christ would return to earth. (The temple that they built there was the same temple that Jeffrey Lundgren many years later planned to seize when doomsday arrived.) Smith also sent followers to Missouri, because he believed that God's New Jerusalem would be built in Independence. Soon afterward, he moved there himself.

From the beginning, the Mormons were not well received in Missouri. The rejection was due, in part, to their unusual religious beliefs—their belief in Moroni and the golden tablets, their desire to build a city where Christ would soon appear, and their certainty that Smith was a prophet. Many folk in Missouri also resented the Mormons' attitude, which some of them found patronizing, as well as their outspoken opposition to slavery, which was widely practiced in Missouri in the 1830s. Nevertheless, by 1833, the Mormons had established a successful community of about ten thousand people in Jackson County.

Fearing the Mormons' growing power and jealous of their wealth, heavily armed neighbors drove Smith and his followers from their homes. When the Mormons resettled elsewhere, their new neighbors forced them out as well. Fearing a violent confrontation and egged on by enemies of the Mormons, the governor of Missouri then ordered all of Smith's followers to leave the state. Their property was confiscated, and Joseph Smith was arrested and tried by a mob. At one point there was talk of executing him.

Joseph Smith founded the Mormon Church.

When Smith was finally freed, he led his followers on to Illinois, where, through incredibly hard work, they established another successful village at Nauvoo. By 1843, more than twenty thousand Mormons were living there. But once again, their neighbors resented them. At the same time, disagreements among the Mormons about how they should live, especially whether men could now take more than one wife, erupted in Nauvoo. These disagreements became violent, and riots swept through the once-peaceful settlement. Enemies outside the village quickly took advantage of the chaos, stirring up trouble between cult members and their neighbors and killing Joseph Smith, the cult's leader. When Smith died, so did his dream of a utopia for the Mormons.

Brigham Young then took over. He led the Mormons to what is now Utah in order to escape persecution. There they founded Salt Lake City. The Mormons, who became—and remain—the majority in Utah, prospered in their new home. Today the Mormon Church has more than 4 million members in the United States, and because it is so large and so successful, many no longer think of it as a cult.

The People's Temple

Although many communes were started in the 1800s (Amana, Zoar, Harmony, Bishop Hill, Bethel, Oneida, Icaria, and Aurora, to mention just a few) and then floundered, the idea of communal living was revived in the 1960s and 1970s, when many young people experimented with different lifestyles. Few communes received more attention in the media than did that of the

Salt Lake City, Utah, looked like this eleven years after the Mormons settled there. Settlers donated a portion of their produce to the Deseret Store, where it was sold. Proceeds supported the church. Brigham Young lived in the large house on the far right.

People's Temple in Jonestown, Guyana. This utopian cult, led by Jim Jones, stunned people all over the world when more than nine hundred members committed group suicide on November 18, 1978.

Jim Jones opened his first church, the People's Temple, in Indianapolis, Indiana, in 1953, when he was twenty-two years old. At first, his congregation was small and poor, so Jones sold pet monkeys door-to-door in order to raise money to pay the church's rent. Jones urged his members to treat all races equally, a position that was not then well received by everyone in Indianapolis. Bigots knocked Jones from his bike as he rode from house to house and tossed dead cats into his church to show their disapproval.

Nevertheless, Jones's congregation grew, notably when the struggle for civil rights began to gain momentum in the late 1950s, not only in Indianapolis but throughout America. About one fourth of his congregation consisted of white, middle-class, well-educated people who were looking for a cause to support. The rest of his congregation was made up of people who had been discriminated against—African Americans, the poor, and the elderly, all of whom were looking for a place to belong.

In 1961, a restless Jim Jones packed up his wife and children and headed for Brazil, where he served as a missionary for two years. While in South America, Jones visited Guyana. This small country, with a history of harboring anyone on the run, would become the site of Jones's utopia thirteen years later.

When Jones returned to the United States in 1963, he resumed leadership in the People's Temple in Indianapolis before moving to California in 1965. Seventy families sold their homes in Indianapolis and followed him to Ukiah, California, a town about one hundred miles north of San Francisco. Before long, Jones had founded churches in San Francisco and Los Angeles.

Reverend Jim Jones attracted lots of attention in California. He operated soup kitchens for the poor and set up nursing homes for the elderly. He also took in prostitutes and drug addicts and helped them turn their lives around. His social programs were so impressive that other churches used Jones's work as an example of what social outreach programs should be.

All went well for Jones until 1977, when former members began to talk about abuse in the People's

Temple. At first, because Jones's reputation was so good, almost everyone doubted the accusations. But two journalists at *New West* magazine, Marshall Kilduff and Phil Tracy, decided to investigate the charges anyway, talking to every former member who would come forward. All told harrowing stories about beatings and being humiliated in front of the congregation. Everything the public had seen was just a front, these members said, designed to get more followers and more money. When asked why no one had spoken out before, former members said that they thought that no one would believe them. Besides, their lives had been threatened by the many armed bodyguards that surrounded Jones.

Jonestown, Guyana

Jones could not tolerate criticism of any kind, so to avoid public humiliation when the *New West* article appeared, he moved to the Temple's utopian settlement he had set up in Jonestown, Guyana. By this time, more than eight hundred followers were living there on leased land. This settlement, begun in 1975, was said to be a tropical paradise where people of all races lived side by side in perfect harmony.

Jones's move did not end the controversy surrounding him, however. More and more former members and families of current members begged Congress to investigate both him and his settlement. Jonestown was not a paradise, these people said, it was a prison.

On November 14, 1978, the investigation began. California's Congressman Leo Ryan, two lawyers, five journalists, and several concerned family members flew to a small airstrip near Jonestown. The delegation received a cool welcome from Jones. Nevertheless, the visitors were given the grand tour. They saw the settlement's school, medical facility, cottages, and agricultural projects, all of which impressed them.

As the investigating committee made the rounds, twenty members of the Temple secretly approached Representative Ryan. They wanted to leave Jonestown, they whispered. Would he help them?

When Ryan agreed to take Jonestown members with him when he left on November 18, and informed Jones that he was doing so, Jones became extremely upset. He felt betrayed as well as threatened. What, he wondered, would the defectors tell the world? Jones then decided to kill the members of the committee and to order his followers to commit mass suicide to try to destroy any incriminating testimony against him.

To get rid of the committee, Jones told several of his loyal followers to accompany the visitors to the airstrip. The loyalists were supposed to shoot the pilot when the plane was in the air so that it would crash, killing everyone aboard. Instead, for reasons not clear, the loyalists decided to kill the visitors on the ground. As the committee began to board one of two planes, the men opened fire, disabling one plane and killing Representative Ryan, three journalists, and one cult member. In addition, several others were wounded. Then, again for reasons not clear, the killers left the scene before finishing their job.

Meanwhile, Jones was lining up nine hundred followers for the mass suicide in Jonestown. It was an unbelievable event, the sounds of which were recorded on tape. As soon as everyone had gathered at the settlement's pavilion, Jones began to speak to them. "I've tried my best to give you a good life. In spite of all that I've tried, a handful of our people, with their lies, have made our life impossible. . . . If we can't live in peace, then let's die in peace."[1]

When Jones stopped speaking, the choir sang a few verses of the hymn *Because of Him*, accompanied by the organ, and Jones's trusted aides began to make the final preparations. The community's doctor and nurses mixed up a huge vat of Flavour-Aid, which they heavily laced with cyanide. And Jones's armed guards made sure that their weapons were loaded.

When the choir stopped singing, Jones spoke again. He told them that the congressman was dead and that it was just a matter of time before the authorities arrived. "The GDF [Guyana Defense Force] will be here. I tell you, get movin', get movin', get movin'. . . . Don't be afraid to die."[2]

The first people to object to the mass suicide, which had been rehearsed more than forty times since the commune had been founded, were shouted down as followers began to move toward the vat. Babies were killed first. Shortly after the poison was poured down their throats, they screamed, their limbs stiffened, and their faces took on grotesque expressions. Nevertheless, mothers and fathers took the same poison once their babies were dead.

But when these adults gasped and writhed in pain, many in line realized that the easy death Jones had promised was anything but, and some refused to participate. A few escaped to the jungle. The rest were murdered.

According to the witnesses, more than one member was physically restrained while being poisoned. A little girl kept spitting out the poison until they held her mouth closed and forced her to swallow it. . . . A woman was found with nearly every joint in her body yanked apart from trying to pull away from the people who were holding her down and poisoning her. All 912 People's Temple members did not die easily.[3]

But all died in less than one hour.

Jones stood watch over the horrible scene almost to the very end, when he was shot dead. No one will ever know for certain if Jones ordered someone to shoot him or if one of his followers took it upon himself or herself to fire the gun. Some have speculated that Jones might have planned to drink the poisoned liquid himself, or even escape into the jungle when the last of his followers was dead.

A Case of Follow the Leader

When news of the deaths in Jonestown reached America, the public was stunned. Why? everyone asked. Why would so many people commit suicide or kill others because someone told them to do so? After a lengthy congressional investigation, some of the reasons became apparent. Most of the people in Jonestown were totally dependent on Jones, and few had the means to escape. His followers had turned over all of their money and their passports to him, making it nearly impossible to leave Guyana. In addition, Jones had forced members to sign blank sheets of paper. He threatened to write confessions

Jim Jones, holding the sign, is showing his support for jailed journalists who refused to reveal their sources. In the early 1970s, Jones was admired for his stand on social issues.

of wrongdoing on these sheets if anyone ever left, and give them to the police. Besides, most of his followers truly believed that he was the Messiah; therefore, they would do anything for him, and if that meant dying or killing, so be it. Heaven, they believed, awaited the faithful, and many were faithful to the end.

5

Help from Beyond: Spiritualist Cults

Margaret and Kate Fox first heard the strange taps on their walls in their Hydesville, New York, home in 1848. Understandably confused when they could not see anyone or anything making these noises, the girls decided to find out what lay behind the puzzling sounds. After tapping on the walls themselves and receiving numerous raps in return, the girls decided that someone was trying to communicate with them. They then devised a system that allowed them to identify the source of the raps: the spirit of a man who had once lived in the Foxes' home. They told many people about this strange occurrence, and a large number of listeners eagerly embraced the girls' story, as proof that a world after death really existed.

Soon other people throughout the country began to hear similar noises in their homes, and these individuals exchanged information. Eventually they met to discuss their beliefs, and Spiritualism was officially born.

This cult had a difficult beginning. At first, the mediums in the group—people who said that they could communicate with the spirits of the deceased—were sought after as people tried to contact friends and family members who had passed away. However, many mediums proved to be little more than frauds, and Spiritualism began to lose believers only a few years after it was started. In 1888, Margaret Fox confessed that she and her sister had lied about the Hydesville rappings, and more followers fell away.

Nevertheless, Spiritualism gained new believers in the 1900s in spite of the continued unmasking of mediums. Today, at least three national organizations exist; the largest is the Universal Church of the Master, which has about ten thousand members. In addition to starting a new faith, Spiritualism laid the groundwork for other cults.

The Ghost Dance Cult

Only a year after Margaret Fox confessed that she and her sister had made up their story, a cult developed in the West that, like other Spiritualist cults of the day, showed members how to reach departed souls. Called the Ghost Dance cult, it spread throughout the Great Plains in 1889 and 1890. Many Native Americans became eager followers, never suspecting that the cult would become the cause of a great tragedy.

The Ghost Dance cult originated with Wovoka, a Paiute prophet in Nevada. Wovoka had numerous visions, and during a particularly vivid one he was taken up into another world. Here he met the spirits of people who had died. He also spoke to God, who told him that all people were supposed to live side by side in peace in order to gain eternal life. God then gave Wovoka directions for the Ghost Dance, a special celebration of peace during which participants could see and talk to those who were in heaven.

Although each tribe changed the dance a little when members adopted it, most followed a general pattern. The dance usually lasted four to six days and began with a twenty-four-hour fast. Men, women, and children participated in the event, some of them wearing special clothing for the occasion, including highly decorated shirts made from white cloth and light buckskin that were known as "ghost shirts." When everyone was ready, the participants gathered and marched in a circle.

A teacher on one of the Sioux reservations, Mrs. Z. A. Parker, observed the dance. She noted that after the participants had marched for a while, they suddenly stopped and "set up the most fearful, heart-piercing wails I ever heard—crying, moaning, groaning, and shrieking out their grief and naming [aloud] their departed friends and relatives. . . . Finally, they raised their eyes to heaven . . . and stood straight and perfectly still, invoking the power of the Great Spirit to allow them to see and talk with their people who had died."[1]

After this, the dancers marched in a circle again, chanting until some participants entered a trance and fell to the ground. The rest then sat down and waited until the dancers regained consciousness and could tell the group what they had seen and heard.

While the dance was spreading from tribe to tribe, stories of two mysterious prophets reached the Great

This illustration of the Ghost Dance was drawn by Dan Smith from sketches made at a Sioux gathering.

Plains. They said that a messiah had finally arrived for the Native Americans; some thought that this savior was Wovoka or even Christ himself. The prophets also predicted that paradise was close at hand; soon, they said, the land would be returned to the tribes and there would be plenty of game and fish. The white men, the stories added, would be swept from the earth.

As the prophecies became better known, the purpose of the dance changed; now, instead of a celebration of peace among all men, the dance became a celebration of the coming paradise. Eager for heaven to arrive, the tribes held more and more dances, believing that by doing so, they were speeding up paradise's arrival.

The increasing number of dances frightened white settlers and Indian agents on the Plains. Both groups thought that the tribes were planning an uprising and that the dances were a way to prepare psychologically for the battles ahead. The agents then asked the army to send more troops to the area as well as to the Sioux reservations in South Dakota, which appeared to be the center of the cult.

After army officials arrived, they decided to arrest Sitting Bull, the leader of the Sioux, in order to put an end to any ideas of an uprising. On December 15, 1890, officials told police officers on the Pine Ridge Reservation, where Sitting Bull lived, to take the leader into custody. A skirmish took place shortly after the officers arrived; Sitting Bull was mortally wounded and several police officers were killed.

Fearing reprisals for the officers' deaths, another Sioux leader, Big Foot, thought it best to take his people away from Pine Ridge to an old camp further west, where he thought that they would be safe. This group of men, women, and children, about 350 altogether, was intercepted by soldiers and told to report to army officials on the Wounded Knee Reservation, which the group did.

When the Sioux arrived at the reservation, soldiers began to disarm them. One warrior refused to surrender his gun, and while he struggled to hold on to it, someone fired a shot. Fearing for their lives, the warriors in the group then tried to retrieve their weapons to defend themselves. To prevent this from happening, the soldiers fired machine guns into the crowd, killing or wounding more than two hundred people, a large number of whom were women and children. This tragedy put to rest the idea that a messiah had come to save the tribes and marked forever the end of the Ghost Dance cult.

The Theosophists Seek Master Spirits

The death of the Ghost Dance cult did not forever end the search for contact with the spiritual world. The Theosophist cult, which was started in the United States in 1875 and sought contact with departed souls, was going strong in 1890, especially in the New England area. Two of the group's founders, Madame Helena Petrovna Blavatsky, a medium from Russia, and Henry Steel Olcott, were studying in India, gathering ideas for their followers from the Hindu and Buddhist faiths. Meanwhile the other founder, William Judge, led the movement in America.

Blavatsky eventually sought guidance from more than the general spirit world. Deeply influenced by Indian religions, she wholeheartedly accepted reincarnation, the belief that upon death, one's spirit is born again in a new body, bringing with it wisdom from previous lives. Blavatsky now tried to find the wisest reincarnated spirits on earth, which were thought to inhabit Eastern religious leaders often known as gurus. In addition, she sought out masters, spirits that had gained so much wisdom and goodness that they were allowed to remain in paradise. She also continued to study all religions, looking for answers to the mysteries of life as well as how to improve human nature.

Madame Blavatsky, a medium from Russia, was one of the founders of the Theosophist Society in the United States.

When Madame Blavatsky died in 1891, Annie Besant, an Englishwoman, took her place. Revolt was already brewing, and small groups then broke away, forming their own Theosophist societies. These groups no longer wanted to be associated with the scandals that surrounded the society. Former members had publicly—and repeatedly—claimed that Blavatsky was a fraud, and later other leaders would be accused of sexual improprieties. Some of the new groups, like the Universal Brotherhood Organization, became very involved in social work, establishing hospitals and schools in California.

The Theosophist movement peaked in the 1920s, when it had about seven thousand members. Even though it was never very large, it had a great influence on other cults. More than one hundred groups can trace their beginnings to the Theosophists, including most New Age cults.[2]

The New Age and Spiritualism

Although Blavatsky often predicted the arrival of a New Age, a paradise on earth brought about because people had become kinder and wiser, it did not happen during her lifetime. The New Age began in the 1970s, when numerous groups combined Eastern and Western religious ideas and then set out to change the human race, one person at a time. To make change possible, these groups emphasized spiritual experiences. The groups varied greatly in their beliefs—some were much more religious than others. All of them, though, relied on some tool or special method to help people connect with the spirits in another world or the source of wisdom inside themselves. These tools and methods included special potions, oils, crystals, magic wands, fortune-telling cards, trances, and yoga.[3] Among the many New Age groups that promoted change through spiritual experiences were Lifespring, Direct Centering, Life Training, Movement of Spiritual Inner Awareness, the Church Universal and Triumphant, and Fellowship of Friends.

New Agers who sought help from the spiritual world wanted to speak to the wisest ones there. One of the most popular ways to receive advice was through "channeling," a process during which a person was taken over by a spirit, who then used the person's voice to communicate with the living.

The New Age movement grew slowly until the 1980s, when the autobiography of actress Shirley MacLaine, *Out on a Limb*, was made into a movie for television. MacLaine, who claimed that her spirit had been reincarnated many times, was swamped with requests from viewers for more information, as were other New Agers. As a result, New Agers held courses, set up shops to sell and share information, appeared on television talk shows, and drew lots of attention to themselves.

They also drew lots of criticism. Some Christian groups saw a conspiracy behind the New Age, a plot concocted by Satan himself to lead people away from the truth. Human beings, these groups said, were simply too sinful to be able to reform themselves. The shocking belief that people could do so without the help of God denied the Bible's most important lessons and put a person's soul in jeopardy. Reporters made fun of the potions, wands, and crystals New Agers thought would help them, their belief in fortune-telling, and the very idea of channeling. Even cartoonists got into the act. For example, Garry Trudeau regularly poked fun at channelers in his cartoon strip, *Doonesbury*. One of Trudeau's characters was often taken over by a spirit from the past, with some comic results.

For a while, though, New Agers could claim that millions of Americans were believers. But when channeling and magic potions failed to bring about the changes New Agers envisioned, membership began to dwindle. Many have regrouped and formed new organizations; others have simply abandoned the dream of a new age on earth.

Scientology and Spirits on Earth

Twenty years before the New Agers began to seek help from the spiritual world, Lafayette Ronald Hubbard, the founder of the Church of Scientology, was developing a method to help spirits on earth. A science fiction writer, Hubbard introduced his program in 1950 in his book *Dianetics: The Modern Science of Mental Health*, which became a best-seller.

Like Blavatsky, and later, many New Agers, Hubbard believed in reincarnation. He also believed that reincarnation was a cause of many mental problems among the living, because the spirit or soul could bring bad memories with it when it entered another body. The moment of reincarnation, Hubbard added, also put into motion what he called the reactive mind, a portion of the mind that recorded negative memories and encouraged people to react to these events in mentally unhealthy ways. This resulted in unhappiness and kept people from attaining their true potential. Hubbard insisted that in order to be happy and successful, bad memories from the past as well as those developed in this lifetime had to be identified and processed.

Identification could be done with a machine that Hubbard invented and patented. Participants were connected to a special meter that measured emotional reactions to painful and embarrassing questions asked by Scientology leaders.

Once problems were identified, participants proceeded to processing. During this stage, believers met with auditors who helped them deal with their emotional pain. This was not only a difficult step, it was also expensive; participants could be charged as much as three hundred dollars per hour for processing, and few could reach the stage of "clear," when no pain registered on the meter, in an hour.

Scientologists have been a source of criticism from the moment they began their church. Some critics doubted Hubbard's credentials for leading a religious movement. Others attacked his methods, his fees, and his beliefs, especially reincarnation and the reactive mind.

Currently there are 7 million people worldwide who have at some time been involved with processing in the Church of Scientology, including some celebrities such as Lisa-Marie Presley, Elvis Presley's daughter. The vast majority of members are in the United States.

Christian Scientists and Spiritual Healing

Scientologists tried to heal ailing spirits. Christian Scientists, on the other hand, sought to heal ailing bodies. This cult was founded in 1875 by Mary Baker

Eddy, a woman who had long been in poor health. During one particularly difficult recovery period, Eddy came to believe that the cause of all illnesses was separation from God, which was brought about by one's weak faith. Therefore, according to Eddy, patients could be healed spiritually by becoming closer to God, strengthening their faith through prayer and study. Eddy then set out to put her ideas into practice. She organized the Christian Science Association, started a school to train practitioners, and opened a church.

Because Christian Scientists refused medical services for illness, they came under attack both from doctors and from the public. Critics argued that the government had a responsibility to protect its citizens, especially children, and that its representatives, such as social workers, should step in if Christian Science members refused to get medical care for themselves or their children. These critics pointed to cases in which children had died because they were denied professional care by their parents. On the other hand, Christian Scientists pointed to a growing list of members whose health had been restored by spiritual healing, arguing that their way was effective.

To date, there have been many court cases involving Christian Scientists who refused medical attention, but there is no clearcut pattern to the decisions. However, in light of the current trend to protect children from abuse, courts have been more willing to order Christian Scientist parents to get medical care for their children or face legal repercussions.

Although the exact number of members belonging to the Church of Christian Science is not made public by the church, it is certain that membership is declining.

This is made clear by the number of churches closing their doors.

The Fearless Snake Handlers

Other cultists who believe that their faith will protect them from physical harm are members of snake-handling cults. Located primarily in small communities in the Appalachian Mountains, these groups long ago formed independent churches. Just as cult members have in the past, today's cultists handle a poisonous snake or drink poison during a special church service as an outward sign of their faith. They believe that they will survive such an ordeal because the Bible tells them so. Cultists quote the sixteenth chapter of Mark, verses fifteen through eighteen, to back their claim:

> Then he [Jesus] said to them: Go forth to every part of the world, and proclaim the Good News to the whole creation. Those who believe it and receive baptism will find salvation; those who do not believe will be condemned. Faith will bring with it these miracles; believers will cast out devils in my name and speak in strange tongues; if they handle snakes or drink any deadly poison, they will come to no harm; and the sick on whom they lay their hands will recover.

If members are bitten (and some have been), they do not seek a doctor's help, believing instead in a spiritual healing. Although over the years not all who have been injured have died, many have lost their lives as a result of testing their faith.

Although the law forbids people to handle poisonous snakes as a test
of their faith, the practice still continues.

Just as in the case of the Christian Scientists, critics
have been appalled at the loss of life. Although snake
handlers have demanded the right to worship as they
please, laws have been passed to outlaw this dangerous
practice, and courts have upheld their constitutionality.
Nevertheless, the practice of handling deadly snakes
continues, and it is likely to do so for many years to
come.

6

Returning to God: Christian Revival Cults

The 1960s and 1970s were marked by great political and social unrest in the United States. Americans were deeply divided over civil rights, student rebellions, the widespread use of drugs, the sexual revolution, and the war in Vietnam. Protesters, especially those opposed to the war, made their feelings known by staging huge demonstrations, some of which turned violent when the police arrived.

The growing number of demonstrations forced Americans to examine their beliefs and values, and many young people, to the horror of their parents, turned their backs on the old ways. Teenager Robert Perez was typical. "I was born into a time when things were in complete chaos," he said. "Everything was breaking down and changing. I was caught up in . . . alternative life-styles."[1] Perez eventually joined a cult.

Thousands of other young adults also joined cults. Some, like Perez, looking for structure and organization in their lives, did so to escape from the rapidly changing world around them; others joined to try to bring about change. In either case, there was no shortage of cults to join, all of which were eagerly seeking members. Many of the newest cults then were led by men who were determined to bring about a massive Christian revival, the likes of which America had never before witnessed.

Reverend Sun Myung Moon

One of the most controversial cults in America in the early 1970s was Reverend Sun Myung Moon's Unification Church, officially known as the Holy Spirit Association for the Unification of World Christianity. The goal of this church was to get Christians to put aside their various denominational differences and unite into one church led by Moon. Like apocalyptic leaders, Moon was eager for Christ's return, but Christ, Moon said, would not return until mankind lived a more righteous life. This was only possible, Moon added, if men and women followed him. He had been told this directly by God, who appeared to him in a vision.

Reverend Moon, a Korean and former Presbyterian, started his first mission in 1948 in North Korea, which was under Communist rule. The Communists denied that any God existed, and they tried to stamp out all religious groups by eliminating their leaders. Moon was arrested, tortured nearly to death, then tossed into an alley to await the burial squad's arrival. Moon's followers found him instead, and they nursed him back to health.

Although Moon was arrested two more times, he managed to build a very loyal following. In the early

1960s, Moon was living and preaching in South Korea, and he had missionaries recruiting members in a number of countries, including the United States.

United States membership grew very slowly until 1972, when Moon moved to America. This marked the beginning of the church's all-out three-year membership drive. In order to finance this drive, followers, often called "Moonies," organized fund-raising activities, selling candles, flowers, and candy door-to-door as well as on busy street corners. These activities were very successful, raising thousands of dollars each week. Most of this money was used to support recruiters who then crisscrossed the country to find new believers. By 1976, Moon claimed to have more than thirty thousand followers in America; other sources believe that the real number was closer to six thousand.

By the middle of the 1970s, Moon's church reported an income of more than $20 million. This money not only supported recruiters, it enabled Moon to buy a twenty-acre estate in New York, which would serve as a theological seminary, an estate for himself, and several money-making properties, such as hotels. Moon used the money from the properties to finance huge rallies designed to attract more believers and to help the poor. Two organizations in Moon's church, Project Volunteer and the Church and Social Action, helped to raise and then distribute food and supplies worth $6 million between 1977 and 1982. Moon's work put him in the public spotlight, and he became a popular figure. He was often seen hobnobbing with important political figures of the day and he was even asked to address Congress.

Critics Take Aim at Moon

Not everyone thought that the Unification Church was a good thing. Critics of Moon attacked the communal lifestyles of his followers. Critics wondered how anyone could be expected to work for twelve to fourteen hours a day, making candles or selling candy, often for no pay other than room and board. In the critics' opinion, this was nothing more than slave labor. Critics also wanted to know how Moon could justify living on a luxurious estate, while his followers lived a very Spartan life, at best. Parents of cult members were appalled at the sight of their children begging people on the street to buy cult products. Furthermore, parents were angered by the fact that many of their children had joined the cult without knowing that it was the Unification Church, for after critics began to

Reverend Sun Myung Moon founded one of the Christian revival cults in the 1970s.

attack the cult, Moon's followers sometimes used a different name when they approached would-be members.

The attacks on Moon mounted over the years, and eventually critics raised so many questions that officials began an investigation into his alleged crimes. In 1982, Moon was charged with income tax evasion, tried, found guilty, and sent to prison for a year. Even though critics hoped that Moon's imprisonment would put an end to the Unification Church, it has failed to do so. At present, there are about four thousand Unification members in the United States.

The Children of God

At the same time that Moon was recruiting followers, dozens of other Christian revival cults were seeking members, including the Way International, the Local Church, and the Children of God. The last cult was founded by David Berg, a former Baptist minister who, like Moon, also had visions. Berg was convinced that America was so sinful that nothing short of a religious revolution could save it. He changed his name to Moses David, in honor of the biblical Moses who led his people to the promised land, replaced the Bible with a series of letters to guide believers, and set out to find followers.

It took Berg nearly ten years to build his cult. He began in the late 1960s, looking for young adults who were so disillusioned with society that they had dropped out, living in small communes or even on the streets. By 1970 he had found enough believers and raised enough money to establish a large commune near Thurber, Texas. He was also able to finance missionaries all over the country. To keep the Children of God in the limelight as much as possible, Berg had cult members dress in long red robes and publicly mourn for America's sins. Often they would walk through cities and towns, chanting or singing hymns as they went along to get attention.

Berg believed that any method of getting people to join his cult was worth using, and he wrote a pamphlet that was full of techniques, which recruiters were required to memorize. Although most recruiters scouted college campuses for potential members, Children of God member Alison Peters searched the malls. She would look for people who looked lost and vulnerable. Then she approached them and, following Berg's pamphlet, tried to gain their trust. "You'd begin by picking on things that you felt were personally interesting to them," she said, "in order to gain their trust. . . . You'd look for the weak spots in people. When the person would bring up something that was uncomfortable for them, you'd use that as an example of how there's so much wrong with the world. . . . You have to play up to the feeling . . . of having no meaning, no sense of real security, no sense of what was going to happen in the future."[2] If verbal persuasion failed, Berg told female recruiters to use "flirty fishing," offering sexual favors when necessary to attract and hold male recruits.[3]

Berg Comes under Fire

Critics of Berg began by attacking his beliefs, especially his ideas regarding proper sexual behavior. Berg, they said, not only promoted prostitution in order to gain members, he told followers to practice unrestricted sex, including adultery and homosexuality, as a sign of love for all people. Berg was also accused of encouraging the sexual abuse of children. Critics hounded Berg and his followers until they decided to leave the country. They established communes in France, Australia, and Brazil. A commune was also started in Spain, where the cult was eventually outlawed. In 1992, some of these believers returned to the United States, prepared to defend themselves against all charges, including child abuse. Currently there are about ten thousand members of the Children of God, which now calls itself the Family of Love or, more often, just the Family.

Changing Minds

Because the lifestyles in Moon's and Berg's cults were so demanding and so different from anything members had experienced previously, curious critics wondered why people remained in the cult for any period of time. When cultists said that they did so because they wanted to and some even described their life in the cult as the happiest that they had ever known, anticultists refused to believe them. Instead, critics decided that cult members had been brainwashed.

"Brainwashing" first became a popular term in the 1950s. It was then that some American servicemen who had been held prisoner by North Koreans during the war between North and South Korea (1950–1953) made startling confessions; the prisoners said that they had fought for the wrong side. The United States was, they insisted, wrong because it was fighting against the Communists, whom the South Koreans really wanted as rulers. The servicemen ended their confessions by announcing that they rejected their American citizenship and planned to spend the rest of their lives in North Korea. These confessions were filmed and used as propaganda to demoralize American soldiers and humiliate the United States.

Government officials and psychologists were quick to argue that these men had not defected of their own free will; instead, they had been forced to commit their traitorous acts. They had been "brainwashed," experts said, by sophisticated techniques recently developed by the Chinese Communists and copied by others, including the Koreans.

Anticult critics compared Korean brainwashing with techniques used by many cults on recruits, insisting that the methods were similar, effective, and harmful. First, victims or recruits were isolated so that they would have few distractions. Prisoners of war were separated from the others being held; cult members were separated from home, family, and friends, as well as from school or the workplace if the cult insisted that new members move into a commune setting. However, even when members were allowed to remain at home, the time-consuming activities expected of the recruits, endless lectures and Bible studies, for example, were so demanding that new members really had no time for their family and former friends. As a result, they were almost as isolated as those in the communes.

Once separation had been achieved, the second stage of brainwashing began. In the prisoner-of-war situation, soldiers were repeatedly lectured to and told to renounce their loyalty to their homeland. To make them more willing to do this, the prisoners were often beaten, starved, and deprived of sleep. Instead of renouncing their homeland, cult recruits were asked to surrender their past lives. Would-be members were expected to attend lengthy lectures, study the leaders' philosophy, and participate in large group sessions during which recruits confessed as many sins in their past as possible. Older members in the cult tried to make recruits feel extremely guilty about these sins. Shame then became a powerful tool that the cult could use to keep members from leaving. How, they asked, could anyone go back to such an awful life? Critics also argued that cult members were deprived of food and sleep as well as time alone to think and reflect, which made them more receptive to the group's beliefs.

The third stage of brainwashing consisted of recruits embracing and even rejoicing in their new lives. Prisoners of war renounced their citizenship and announced their plans for the future, including living in a new homeland. Cult members usually sold all that they had and gave it to the cult's leader as proof that their old life was over. Some took a new name.

All eagerly professed to having a very different view of the world from the one they had before entering the cult. As one member of Moon's cult said, "I felt I had found my 'home' at last. . . . I felt *completely* carefree for the first time in my life and [I experienced] a feeling of great hope for the future, not just for myself but for the whole world."[4]

Doubters

The idea that someone could really be brainwashed came under fire by many psychologists in the 1980s; most doubted that it was possible to force people to radically change their beliefs for any length of time, unless the recruits really wanted to change. These experts pointed out that throughout history soldiers had defected in wars and that they were doing so long before brainwashing techniques were used. In addition, the vast majority of cult members left the cult shortly after joining. Some experts estimate that only 10 percent of cult members remain longer than two years. Furthermore, in a study done by Eileen Barker as part of her research for her book *The Making of a Moonie: Choice or Brainwashing?* Barker found that only a fraction of the people who were interested in joining Moon's cult and attended lectures were members two years later.[5] If brainwashing was as powerful as critics claimed, doubters asked, why didn't all prisoners of war renounce their citizenship? How could any cult member ever leave the group? How could anyone who was interested in a cult be able to leave the premises after visiting with members? Besides, weren't the techniques (isolation, indoctrination, acceptance of new ideals) similar to those used by convents, monasteries, and even the armed services? And didn't society accept and even applaud these institutions? How, then, could these methods be called harmful?

But even though doubters raised questions about brainwashing, many people continued to believe that it was possible to change someone's mind, if not by brainwashing, then by using mind control, which uses isolation and indoctrination but not physically violent acts. In short, anticultists still saw—and continue to see—cults as dangerous organizations.

7

A Foreign Influence: Cults from the East

Early one morning in 1978, members of a Hare Krishna community in West Virginia had just begun their worship service when heavily armed intruders charged into the Krishnas' temple. After firing several shots to frighten the worshippers, the gunmen forced the Krishnas to destroy statues of their gods and threatened the group's leader. Then the intruders quickly withdrew from the scene. The Hare Krishnas, badly shaken by the incident, feared more attacks in the future. They were right about more assaults, but these would come from temple members, not local thugs.

Originally, this Krishna community had been part of a nationwide Hare Krishna organization that was started in India by Swami Prabhupada (swamis are Hindu religious teachers) and brought to the United States in 1965. However, in 1987, the West Virginia community withdrew its group from the national cult. The decision to separate was the result of disagreements about how the national organization should be run, not basic religious beliefs, for the Krishnas in West Virginia continued to share the same faith.

The Hare Krishnas' Beliefs

The cult's founder, Swami Prabhupada, expected followers to lead a simple life of total devotion to Krishna, an all-powerful Hindu god. Members were required to sever ties with friends and family and move into communes. In most cases, the communes were farms where followers raised their own food for their vegetarian diets. American Krishnas, like their counterparts in India, often went barefoot, wore long gowns or pajama-like outfits, and shaved their heads. Most of the members' days were spent worshipping their god and seeking a state of bliss. To find this state, followers entered trances through intense concentration, helped along by chanting "Hare Krishna, Hare Krishna." Some cult members were immigrants from India, who, now that American immigration restrictions against Asians had been modified, could enter the United States in greater numbers. Most, however, were young Americans looking for an alternative lifestyle during the especially turbulent times of the 1960s and 1970s.

Criticisms and Controversy

Many of the cult's first recruits were young adults who had serious drug problems. Prabhupada and his followers had sought out these addicts and rehabilitated them. This won public approval.

A number of American cults started in the 1970s had their beginnings here, in India.

But when the cult reached out to all, eagerly pursuing members everywhere, Americans became deeply concerned, then hostile. Part of this hostility was due to recruiting and fund-raising techniques. Hare Krishnas handed out pamphlets about their beliefs and sold flowers in public places, especially busy airports, to raise money for the cult. Because members were very aggressive, citizens began to complain about being harassed or, at the very least, annoyed by the Krishnas and their strange clothing and chanting.

Although hostility on the part of the public toward the Krishnas continued to increase throughout the 1970s, membership in the cult grew. By the end of the decade, the cult had fifty centers in the United States. It was also operating a small number of successful vegetarian restaurants and earning more than $2 million a year in its incense business, which sold fragrant kindling and oils meant to perfume the air when burned. Critics, especially the fearful parents of children in the cult, leveled charges of deception, brainwashing, and enticement of minors against the Krishnas.

Some of these charges gained national attention. One case involved Robin George, who joined the cult when she was a minor. George's parents publicly threatened to take their daughter home, using force if necessary, and the Krishnas responded by moving Robin from center to center in an unsuccessful attempt to hide her. In another case, a divorced mother who did not have legal custody of her son, David Yanoff, took him with her when she joined the cult. When David's father came looking for him, the Krishnas repeatedly moved the boy for over a year before surrendering him.[1]

At about the same time, the Krishnas in West Virginia were accused of dealing in drugs to raise money. A few members had reverted to their old ways, and they were caught bringing drugs into the country by hiding them in religious statues sent from abroad. This did little to endear any Krishnas to the public.

But the real blows to the organization, especially the group in West Virginia, came from within. In October 1985, the leader of the West Virginia commune was shot and seriously wounded by one of the group's members. Soon afterward, another West Virginia cult member, Thomas Dresher, was charged with murder. Then, in

1990, two West Virginia cult leaders were accused of illegal fund-raising practices; one of them was found guilty. While he awaited the results of his appeal he was released on bail.[2] The resulting publicity surrounding these crimes and trials drove out many members and seriously hampered recruiters' efforts to find replacements. Today, there are fewer than five thousand Hare Krishnas in the United States.

The Divine Light Mission

Another cult with a decidedly Eastern influence that flourished during the 1970s was the Divine Light Mission. This cult was started in India in 1960. It was based upon beliefs that had been popular throughout much of northern India since the 1920s—that there is a succession of spiritual masters on earth, each one an embodiment of God and therefore worthy of worship, who can help followers find truth and an explanation of the meaning of life.

When the founder died in 1966, his youngest son, Maharaj Ji, who was only eight years old, assumed leadership. Because Maharaj Ji was so young, his mother and older brother helped him shoulder his responsibilities. When he was thirteen years old, he decided to take the Divine Light Mission's message to America. His mother and brother, who were opposed to this move, remained in India.

At first, the Divine Light Mission flourished in the United States as had no other cult. Within a few years of Maharaj Ji's arrival, mission leaders claimed a following of over fifty thousand.

This phenomenal growth was due to several factors. First, the mission had a number of American supporters long before Maharaj Ji arrived, most of them young adults who had traveled in India and had been impressed with the mission movement there. Second, many members held outside jobs that paid well, and these members gave a percentage of their salaries to the cult, providing it with a reliable income. Also, the mission's projects, helping the poor and running health clinics, genuinely appealed to idealistic young people of the day.

But the mission, like all cults, was not without its critics. It was accused of brainwashing and deceiving its members. And many critics ridiculed the mission's teenage leader, who, they said, showed few signs of great wisdom or any ability to preach or lead.

Trouble Within the Cult

Maharaj Ji's loyal followers began to desert him barely three years after he arrived in America. Many became upset when he, at age sixteen, married his twenty-four-year-old secretary and moved into a luxurious home financed by the mission. Among those most distressed by his marriage was Maharaj Ji's mother, who disowned him. He eventually took his mother to court in India, to be made the legal head of the mission in India. Maharaj Ji's mother argued that he showed poor judgment and was therefore unfit for any leadership position. The ugly legal battles and family fight that ensued further damaged the mission's image in the United States. By 1980, most centers had been closed. The name of the organization was then changed to Elan Vital, and Maharaj Ji, who seldom appears in public, is still the group's leader.

The Rajneesh Foundation International

A third cult that started in India and was brought to the United States was the Rajneesh Foundation International, founded by Bhagwan (godman) Rajneesh in 1966. Rajneesh, a philosophy instructor and a follower of Jainism, a faith whose members believe in reincarnation, had several visions in 1953 that deeply affected him. He started speaking to people about his new beliefs, reinterpreting old Jainist sacred writings in a way that shocked the religion's scholars, because he did not believe that its followers had to withdraw from the sinful world and lead a monastic life in order to worship properly. Despite being criticized, by 1974 Rajneesh had gathered enough followers and funds to start a commune in India.

In 1981, after his commune was destroyed by fire—arson was suspected—Rajneesh and some of his followers moved to the United States. The foundation purchased sixty-four thousand acres of land near Antelope, Oregon, where Rajneesh planned to build Rajneeshpuram, a model community that would, if all went as planned, eventually house thousands of followers. In the summer of 1982, seven thousand supporters flocked to the area for a festival.

Controversy in Antelope

Although Rajneesh had had his share of criticism in India, it did little to prepare him for the hostility that he encountered in Oregon. Environmentalists and local

81

landowners were appalled by his plans to build a community. They wanted open spaces and peace and quiet, not a growing—and controversial—cult next door. Even so, members began to build.

Rajneesh and his followers then decided that in order to expand their community, they would need political clout. They petitioned officials of Antelope, asking them to make the community part of the town, a request that was finally granted. Once part of the town, cult members ran for office, and because they had many votes, they were able to capture the majority of seats on the city council. In addition, one of their members was elected mayor. Outnumbered townspeople were enraged by the results of the election, believing that they had lost their voice in their own town.

As controversy over the foundation continued to grow, local authorities looked for some way to eliminate the cult. Eventually, immigration officials discovered that some of the members' immigration papers, including Rajneesh's, were not in order. Rajneesh was arrested and fined. He returned to India. The land in Oregon was sold, and cult members scattered across the United States, forming small centers of their own. There are currently about thirty-seven centers in the United States.

The Black Muslims

A fourth cult with an Eastern background, the Black Muslims, not only gained national attention during the 1960s, but continues to make headlines today. Officially known as the Nation of Islam, this cult was founded in Detroit, Michigan, in 1930 by Wallace D. Fard, a mysterious man who called himself the Supreme Ruler of the Universe.

Fard told his followers that blacks were the original inhabitants of the earth, and that they had founded the ancient city of Mecca, the center of the Nation of Islam in what is now Saudi Arabia, thousands of years ago. African Americans, Fard argued, had become separated from the Nation of Islam by white devils (slave traders), descendants of the first whites who were created by a mad scientist about six thousand years ago. These white devils had wreaked havoc on blacks throughout the world. It was time, Fard said, for African Americans to be reunited with their true religion.

Wallace Fard met with small groups of potential followers in their homes. When they decided to join his cult, they gave up their American names and took Muslim names instead. Some followers put an "X" after their new first name to indicate that they were descendants of slaves, who, because their ancestors had been forced to abandon their family names when they were enslaved, had lost their true identity.

Fard vanished in 1934. No proof of foul play was ever uncovered, nor was he ever heard from again, and his disappearance remains a mystery. Elijah Muhammad became the leader of the Black Muslims. Membership grew slowly and there was little publicity until Malcolm X arrived on the scene in the late 1950s. Malcolm X, the leader of the Harlem mosque, one of the most important Muslim congregations, was both dynamic and outspoken, and his comments enraged and frightened white Americans. Malcolm X told African Americans that they should reject all white men's religions, especially

Christianity. "This white man's Christian religion," he said, "deceived and brainwashed [African Americans] to always turn the other cheek, and grin, and scrape, and bow, and be humble, and to sing, and to pray and to take whatever was dished out by the devilish white man."[3]

Malcolm X wanted a better life for his followers. The civil rights movement had not yet picked up steam, and African Americans were discriminated against everywhere: in schools, on the job, in housing units, and even on buses, where they had to sit in the back. When Malcolm X said that he had had enough of such treatment and wanted a separate homeland—eight or more states—for African Americans, the public became alarmed. When Malcolm X said that he would use force if necessary to achieve his goals, the public shuddered.

Malcolm X's Assassination

Malcolm's comments eventually alarmed Black Muslim leaders as well, and some of these leaders refused to support him. In 1963, Malcolm X left the Black Muslims. Some sources claim that Malcolm X was expelled; others insist that he resigned. In either case, the split was both final and bitter.

Shortly after, Malcolm X started a new organization, the Muslim Mosque. Now, in addition to attacking white devils, he also attacked the Black Muslims, who, he said, had fallen away from the true faith. Within a few months, Malcolm X began to receive death threats, and in February 1965, he was assassinated by a Black Muslim.

Malcolm X was a controversial leader of the Black Muslims in the 1960s.

Fighting then broke out between the Black Muslims and Malcolm X's Muslim Mosque. Members of both groups were brutally attacked, and even murdered.

Louis Farrakhan

In 1995, the public's attention was once again focused on the Black Muslims and their very vocal leader, Louis Farrakhan. The comments of Farrakhan, who had replaced Malcolm X as the leader of the Harlem mosque, had already made numerous headlines. He lashed out at many groups, verbally attacking Jews, Koreans, Palestinian Arabs, and homosexuals in particular, and all whites in general. His remarks, like those of Malcolm X, deeply upset the public, and even though most people were repulsed by what Farrakhan said, he continued to spew forth hatred and bigotry.

Lately, however, Farrakhan, who has given up the idea of a separate nation for African Americans, claims that he will use peaceful means to improve the lives of his followers. Farrakhan hopes to make the Black Muslims a powerful religious and political force that will speak for Black America. His first nationwide attempt at unifying the Black community was the "Million Man March," in which African-American men from all over America met in Washington, D.C., in October 1995, to celebrate their ancestry, demonstrate their solidarity, and pledge to improve themselves "spiritually, morally, mentally, socially, politically and economically."[4] Although criticized because it did not include African-American women, this march was very successful. It put Farrakhan in a more positive light than before. However, many critics doubt that he has abandoned his old beliefs or his attitude of prejudice. He currently has twenty thousand followers. Whether they can become a powerful force remains to be seen.

8

It's Magic: Witchcraft and Voodoo Cults

Nine-year-old Betty Parris was the first to be afflicted in the Puritan village of Salem, Massachusetts, in January 1692. For hours at a time, this once-active girl simply sat in a chair and stared straight ahead. She also refused to eat, made strange animal-like noises, and would burst into tears for no apparent reason.

Betty's eleven-year-old cousin, Abigail Williams, who lived with the Parris family, was next. Abigail would suddenly drop to her hands and knees and bark like a dog or race about the house with her arms flapping as if she were trying to fly. These actions greatly upset Reverend and Mrs. Parris, who were understandably puzzled by the girls' strange behavior. The Parrises' confusion turned to terror when Abigail told them that she saw "shapes," ghost-like images of witches, in the Parrises' living room. The mere mention of shapes was proof to a Puritan that a witch was at work in the village, trying to find souls for the Devil.

Soon, the Parrises learned that girls in two other Salem households had similar symptoms. Dr. Griggs, who had been asked to diagnose the girls, announced that they had been bewitched. In addition, he said that none of the girls would get better until the witch who was afflicting them was found.

So the Salem witch hunt began, one of the most famous searches for witches in the world. It was brought to a halt in late 1692 by the governor of the Massachusetts Bay colony, Sir William Phips. By that time, at least forty people had claimed that they had seen shapes and had therefore been bewitched, one hundred fifty citizens were in jail awaiting trial, and nineteen suspects had been tried, convicted, and put to death.

Historians have long debated the causes of the Salem witchcraft trials; most, however, believe that mass hysteria was a major factor. The girls had been trying out a little witchcraft themselves in order to predict their futures, and they feared that their actions had set loose evil forces in the village. The girls' terror caused their physical symptoms, and those symptoms convinced the villagers that witches were committing dastardly deeds with their supernatural powers. So the villagers of Salem entered into the hunt with zeal and determination. Because an accused witch could save his or her life by confessing and then naming other witches, the temptation to provide a name or two was great. As a result, more and more suspects were rounded up and thrown into jail.

The Devil's Servants

The colonists' belief that witches were working for the Devil was based upon a book titled *Malleus Maleficarum* (The Witch Hammer), which was published in 1486 by two Christian priests. Until this book appeared, witches, who worshipped gods and goddesses associated with nature, were not thought to be a threat to anyone's soul, although historically they were blamed for many ills on earth, such as raging storms or droughts. *Malleus Maleficarum* argued that witches were more than just a threat on earth; they were the Devil's servants who were out to snatch Christian souls, thereby damning them to hell for all eternity. According to the two priests, all witches had made a deal with Satan. He gave them power; in return, the witches found followers for the Devil, pestering and plaguing good people until they agreed to worship him. The authors supported their case with recent confessions taken from men and women accused of witchcraft who had been beaten and tortured with hot irons to get them to tell the "truth" about their relationship with Satan.

Witches were therefore intolerable, the authors said, and they had to be eliminated. To make sure that witches could no longer work their black magic, and to deter others from following Satan, witches were burned to death—slowly—at the stake. Sometimes, especially if a witch was really old, the executioners would take pity and behead the victim so that death would be quick and then burn the remains over a roaring fire. Eventually, hanging became the preferred form of execution. No one knows for sure how many witches were killed in Europe and

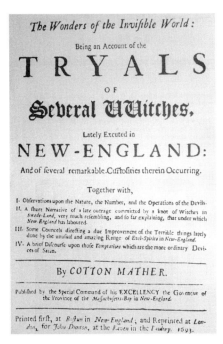

Cotton Mather was a famous Puritan minister in the late 1600s and an avid witch hunter. He published this pamphlet about witchcraft in 1693 to keep colonists informed about the Devil's helpers.

America during the witch hunts; estimates run from tens of thousands into the millions.[1]

According to popular colonial belief, witches in America were just as bad as their counterparts in Europe. Not only were they claiming souls, but they held wild, evil celebrations late at night in secret meeting places deep in the woods. Celebrants donned black robes, if they wore anything at all, danced in the most disgraceful manner, sang off-key, shouted obscenities, and feasted on human flesh. If the celebration was particularly wicked, the Devil himself would appear. When the festivities ended, witches mounted their broomsticks for a quick flight home, their long stringy hair flying in the wind. This colonial image of witches still lives, and this makes modern-day witches very angry.

Modern Witchcraft Cults

One of the founders of modern-day witchcraft was Gerald B. Gardner, a British civil servant who worked in Asia for many years. Gardner was intrigued by the religions he encountered while on assignment, especially those that used magic. He gathered all the information about magic that he could while he was in Asia and when he returned to England, he started adding to it. Most of the information he sought at home, however, no longer existed; it had been lost or destroyed when witchcraft was outlawed in Great Britain centuries before. When the ban on witchcraft was lifted in 1951, Gardner published a handbook of spells. He also started his own coven, a group of witches with whom he developed many witchcraft rituals. Although he tried to reconstruct ancient witchcraft, which may have been one of the earliest religions on earth, he was unable to do so, because so much information had been lost over the centuries. As a result, what Gardner created was really a new form of witchcraft, Wicca.

Witches from England brought Wicca to the United States in 1962. Shortly after, small covens were established in America. At least two groups grew out of Wicca; one was started by Alexander Sanders and another by Sybil Leek. Other groups were also organized that were not associated with Wicca but held similar beliefs. Some of these independent groups called themselves NeoPagans (new non-Christians). Today, about forty thousand North Americans belong to Wicca and NeoPagan groups. Because Wicca is a religion, members insist that the term "Witch" be capitalized, as is the term "Methodist," or "Catholic," or "Muslim."

The most common form of execution for witches in Europe was burning at the stake. In the colonies, most witches were hanged.

Modern Witches share a number of beliefs and practices. They worship the Great Mother Goddess, often called Diana, as well as a variety of other deities, all of whom are associated with nature. Witches practice two varieties of magic: low magic, designed to improve one's immediate situation, such as finding a better job; and high magic, designed to change an individual. Although some Witches claim to have supernatural powers, many do not. One Witch, Leo Martello, said, "I make no claims as a [W]itch to 'supernatural powers,' but I totally believe in the *super* powers that reside in the *natural*."[2] Witches also seek to control the forces within themselves that make life possible in order to live wisely and well and in harmony with nature. They promise to harm no one, for they believe that if they do, the harm they bring about will return to them—threefold.

Because Witches have not been able to shake the old image of being the Devil's helpers, they have not been well received in many communities. Not long after Wicca had arrived in the United States, a coven was organized near Dimmitt, Texas. Townspeople objected to the coven, and some harassed the group's leaders, Louise and Loy Stone, by driving around the Stones' home, shouting their objections. On Halloween, 1977, Loy Stone felt so threatened that he shot at a group who had become especially abusive, wounding one member of the group and killing another. Stone was arrested for murder, tried, and found not guilty; the jury believed that he had acted in self-defense.[3]

More recently, the largest Witchcraft-NeoPagan organization, located near Madison, Wisconsin, ran into stiff resistance when the organization's leader tried to expand the group's facilities. When a building permit was denied, the group's leader took the dispute to court, where she won.

Although it is risky to do so, some Witches have decided to become more visible. They are appearing on talk shows and publishing newsletters, both to keep in touch with their members and to educate the public. There are at least thirty such publications in circulation today. Witches are also becoming more politically active. A coven in California that is especially vocal on political issues is named after Susan B. Anthony, one of America's most famous suffragettes.

More Magic—Voodoo

Like Witches, practitioners of Voodoo also believe in magic. The first people to practice Voodoo in what is now the United States were slaves who were brought to New Orleans, Louisiana, in the early 1700s. Other slaves from Africa as well as former slaves from Haiti added their rituals over the years, and a special form of magic evolved, New Orleans Voodoo.

Women played an important part in the new Voodoo, just as they did in witchcraft. In fact, one of the most famous and controversial Voodoo practitioners was Marie Laveau, who set up shop in New Orleans in the mid-1800s. She gained quite a reputation over the years as bad things often happened to the people she cursed— and many came to fear her. Today, believers still go to her grave, where they hope to get help. They mark her grave-stone with "X" symbols that, according to legend, will give visitors special powers.

Witches were thought to have extraordinary powers over nature. In this old illustration they are shown stirring up a storm.

Voodoo spells, or hexes, were cast for good or evil. Believers could request that a priestess cast a spell that would bring them good luck. This was called White Voodoo. Applicants would be expected to carry a charm, a rabbit's foot or a monkey's paw, for example, until the hex took effect. Black Voodoo, such as putting a curse on someone, also required a physical symbol. Often the intended victims would be sent tiny black caskets to announce the curse and scare them out of their wits.

New Orleans Voodoo is still practiced, but it is difficult to determine just how many people participate in it. Many believers in this cult prefer to keep a low profile to avoid harassment.

Santería

One type of Voodoo, however, is becoming more public, and this is Santería. The foundations of this cult in the Western Hemisphere date from the early 1800s when slaves from Nigeria were brought to Cuba to work on the island's sugar plantations. These slaves continued to worship their old gods, but they also adopted some Roman Catholic beliefs, adding them to their Voodoo practices. In the process, they created an unusual mix that flourished. In 1959, Fidel Castro forced thousands of Cubans to flee when he became the dictator of Cuba. Many of the refugees came to the United States, bringing Santería with them.

They have been joined over the years by other Cuban refugees, notably in 1980 when Castro, trying to eliminate his growing number of enemies, allowed many of them to leave the country. Thousands moved into Cuban communities throughout Florida as well as in New York City and Chicago, Illinois. Although the exact number of Santería cultists is not known, the number of shops that sell herbs and other materials used in Santería ceremonies is growing rapidly. There are now at least one hundred of these stores in Miami, Florida, and one hundred twenty Santería suppliers in New York City alone.

Santería practices, especially the practice of sacrificing animals at worship services, angered animal rights supporters as well as cult neighbors. Santería members worship *orisha*, or spirits, which descend during religious services. These spirits help followers predict the future and therefore are eagerly sought after. One way to attract them is to sacrifice animals. After an animal, usually a chicken, is killed, it is cooked and eaten by worshippers.

Although neighbors complained for years about the animal sacrifices, little was done to stop the practice. But in 1987, when Ernesto Pichardo leased a used-car lot and building in Hialeah, Florida, that was to be used as a site for Santería worship services, townspeople decided that they had had enough. Pichardo had publicly admitted that he had lost count of the number of animals that he had sacrificed—thousands, he thought—and most of the townspeople were upset at the very sight of the man. They then began a petition drive to stop Pichardo, and the city's leaders responded by passing a string of ordinances that, if followed, would have severely weakened Santería's rituals.

Pichardo was enraged by the new ordinances, and he went to court to fight them. He argued that the townspeople were hypocrites. "You can kill a turkey in your backyard, put it on the table, say a prayer and serve it for Thanksgiving," he said. "But if we pray over the turkey, kill it, then eat it, we violated the law."[4] Two lower courts supported the townspeople; however, the United States Supreme Court, in July 1993, ruled in favor of the Santería church, thereby ending what had become known as the "Chicken Wars." It is highly unlikely that this is the end of persecution for the Santería cult, though. Like Witches, Santería members have a poor image in the public's eye, and this will lead to more difficulties for cult members in the future.

9

Worshipping the Devil: Satanic Cults

Over the years, many stories about cults have taken their emotional toll on the public. Americans were deeply upset when they witnessed the deaths of the Branch Davidians, horrified by the Jonestown suicides, and incensed by the likes of Charles Manson and his Family. None, however, has caused as much emotional turmoil as have Satanic cults.

Many Americans believe in the Devil. In a recent poll, almost 60 percent of the people questioned said that the Devil exists. Some thought that Satan was a supernatural being; others said that he was a powerful, impersonal force.[1]

According to Christian beliefs, the Devil has brought about great pain and anguish. In fact, he introduced sin into the world when he persuaded Eve to eat the forbidden apple in the Garden of Eden. Since then he has repeatedly succeeded in tempting others to do evil things.

This perception has been reinforced by famous and not-so-famous criminals who have sometimes said that they committed their crimes because they were Devil worshippers. It is not surprising, then, that anyone claiming to worship Satan would be feared and despised, not only by Christians, but by the public in general. Everyone has a stake in the crime rate.

Traditional Satanic Cults

How many people have actually worshipped the Devil since ancient times is impossible to determine. If large numbers of worshippers have existed, they have kept their activities a well-guarded secret; confessions from tortured men and women suspected of Devil worship, such as accused witches, are hardly reliable sources, and no written records have been found.

It is also very difficult to find reliable information about ancient Satanic services and rituals such as the infamous Black Mass. In fact, although Satanists have been credited with starting this parody of a Catholic Mass, the Black Mass may actually have been a bizarre creation of Catherine de Medici, the wife of King Henry II of France. When Henry died in 1559, Catherine is said to have written a special service for him in which the Catholic Mass was read backward, and the altar was topped with a naked girl.[2]

People who attended the mass were so intrigued by it that they held their own services just for the fun of it, and Black Masses became an upper-class fad. As more and more people participated in these masses, other elements were added. For example, participants served black bread

99

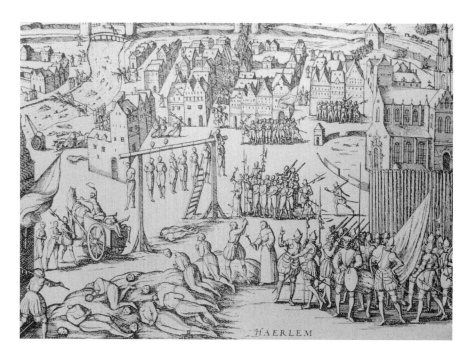

Suspected Satanists have been persecuted for hundreds of years. For example, in 1573, the Duke of Alba, a military leader in Spain, executed many citizens in Haerlem, Netherlands, believing that they were disciples of the Devil.

instead of white wafers, which Roman Catholics used, at "communion" services.

Another ritual Satanists were supposed to practice was human sacrifice. According to an enduring rumor, known as the blood ritual myth, Devil worshippers kidnapped children and sacrificed them during a Black Mass. Interestingly enough, the blood ritual rumor has been used against more than one group in history. In the first century A.D., the Romans accused the first Christians of sacrificing Roman children, in an effort to discredit the new cult. All through the Middle Ages, Christians accused Jews of kidnapping and killing Christian children, in order to justify driving out Jews from their towns and villages. And in the fifteenth century, French peasants used to say that rich noblemen killed poor children in order to use their blood for baths. In most cases, the blood ritual myth has surfaced during times of great stress, serving as a scapegoat, the supposed source of all problems.

Besides mocking masses and sacrificing children, Satanic cults have been accused of almost every evil act imaginable. Even so, only a few cases have been documented, and these involved teenagers who had a long record of drug abuse. One of the first Satanic cults to receive national attention made headlines in the 1970s when a cult member asked his friends to help him kill himself. He thought that after his death he would return to earth as a leader of demons. In 1984, a Long Island cult shocked the public when members killed one of their own. Members of the media speculated that the death was a sacrifice to Satan. Several years later, another Satanic cult killed a member in Sacramento, California. None of these groups was associated with other cults, and as they were unable to find reliable records, members simply made up what they thought would be proper Satanic rituals.

A Network of Satanic Cults?

Although there have been few documented Satanic cults in America, the public believes that many exist and may even be part of a national network. This belief is due to at least three factors. First, popular music groups have included references to Devil worship in their songs and used Satanic symbols on album covers. As a result, the ideas and symbols thought to be associated with Satanism seem to be everywhere. Second, popular talk shows with nationwide audiences, such as *Geraldo*, have featured numerous programs about Satanic cults. And third, some cult experts, who make a very good living giving seminars on Satanism, keep telling Americans that Satanic groups are at work everywhere. These experts allege that there are at least 2 million members of Satanic cults in America today.[3]

Satanic Panic

Because of the commonly held belief that Satanic cults are widespread, rumors about such cults are readily believed no matter where they begin, and they have been started in every part of the country. In New York State, rumors of Satanic cult activity included a planned sacrifice of a blonde-haired, blue-eyed child on Halloween, a Satanic holy day. This rumor grew out of some new graffiti in town that contained symbols associated with Satanism. When three teens were arrested for the vandalism, the boys said that their use of the symbols was nothing more than a prank and insisted that they were not Devil worshippers. In Indiana, rumors about the possible kidnappings of children began to circulate after a local cemetery was vandalized. Later, the same rumors were heard in a nearby community. In fact, in the last ten years, blood ritual myths have repeatedly surfaced in Alabama, Arizona, Colorado, Georgia, Idaho, Illinois, Indiana, Iowa, Kansas, Kentucky, Mississippi, Montana, New Mexico, North Carolina, North Dakota, Ohio, Oklahoma, Pennsylvania, Virginia, West Virginia, Wisconsin, and Wyoming. In all of the states the rumors were believed, but in no state did a kidnapping or Satanic sacrifice actually take place.[4]

Satanic Ritual Abuse

In the 1980s, another form of blood ritual myth began to circulate: In addition to being sacrificed, children were being sexually abused by Satanic cults. The first person to make such an accusation was Michelle Smith. Smith's story became well-known when her psychiatrist, Lawrence Pazder, published a book titled *Michelle Remembers*, which was based upon events Michelle recalled under hypnosis. Smith said that she was assaulted for about a year, beginning in 1954, by a cult of Satanists to which her parents belonged, in Victoria, British Columbia. Michelle claimed that:

> She witnessed babies and adults being ritually killed and butchered and that she was even fed ashes from the burned remains of a victim. On another occasion, Michelle claim[ed] that a fetus was sliced in half in front of her and then rubbed on her body. She claim[ed] that she was frequently kept naked in a special cage that was sometimes filled with snakes

103

[and] she was tied up and a mass of little red spiders was made to crawl over her and bite her. . . . The culmination of Michelle's torture came when Satan himself visited the rituals.[5]

Dr. Pazder, who was treating Michelle and who wrote *Michelle Remembers*, believed strongly in his patient's story. He also had an unshakable belief in Satanism. Pazder had witnessed a number of black magic ceremonies while he was a doctor in West Africa, and he had taken photographs of these rituals. Critics of the case think that Pazder's beliefs preconditioned him to accept Smith's story and that in turn his photos gave Michelle ideas about what a Satanic cult ritual might involve.

Whatever its source, Smith's story served as a model, and in the next few years numerous accounts of Satanic cult abuse were published or described in detail on televised talk shows. Many victims recalled being impregnated in order to provide babies for ritual sacrifices. In most cases, the young women telling the stories clearly appeared to be suffering as they related their horrible ordeals, all of which had been forgotten or repressed until recently.

At first these stories were eagerly sought after, widely read, and believed by many citizens. Supporters argued that the various accounts were consistent—victims recounted the same sorts of abuse all over the country. This, supporters said, proved that a nationwide Satanic organization existed.

However, when the victims' stories were checked, not a single shred of evidence—dead bodies, secret rooms where the abuse took place, burial sites, or even one witness who could recall a victim's pregnancy—could be found. In one famous case, Lauren Stratford, who wrote *Satan's Underground*, was publicly called a liar for claiming that she had been repeatedly abused by a Satanic cult.[6] In fact, doubters of Stratford's story pointed out that Lauren could not prove any of her charges and that she had a well-known habit of lying, having posed in the past as a drug addict, a prostitute, and a blind person in order to get attention. Stratford's reputation and her failure to convince critics cast doubt not only on her story, but on other stories about Satanic abuse as well.

Another factor that made the public question these claims of Satanic abuse was the similarity of the victims' accounts to a rash of stories about abuse in Catholic convents that had surfaced in the 1830s and 1840s. One of the most popular, *The Awful Disclosures of Maria Monk*, was written by a young woman who had entered a convent in Montreal, Canada, in order to be educated. She claimed to have witnessed scenes of rape, torture, and murder that were very similar to those described by Michelle and other victims of Satanic abuse.[7] These books were published at a time when anti-Catholicism was strong in America, and many people took them seriously even though the stories were subsequently proved to be false.

The Latest Victims

At the same time that Michelle Smith and other victims were coming forward, hundreds of children began to tell blood-curdling stories about Satanic abuse in day-care centers. The first case to receive national attention began in August 1983 in Manhattan Beach, California, where Judy Johnson claimed that her son had been sexually molested at the McMartin Preschool. Johnson, who had serious emotional and health problems, added vivid details to the sexual assault case over the coming weeks. She also made some new charges, insisting that a Marine regularly went to the school and sexually abused the children there and that staff members had tortured her son by repeatedly jabbing scissors into his eyes. Johnson even accused Peggy McMartin Buckey of sacrificing a baby and forcing Johnson's son to drink the baby's blood.[8]

Johnson's charges caused a hysterical reaction among other parents of children in the same school and led to an intensive investigation. More than three hundred children who at some time had attended the preschool were questioned, and Peggy McMartin Buckey and her son, Ray, were charged with more than one hundred counts of child molestation.

The stories the children told were incredible. Shortly after being dropped off in the morning, they said, they had been flown to secret sites where everyone worshipped the Devil. Some had been dragged to a secret room beneath the school, where they had been tortured and animals had been sacrificed. Teachers had dressed like witches or had worn nothing at all as they flew on broomsticks back and forth across the room.

It took years to resolve this case, and a final decision was not reached until January 1990, when the Buckeys were found not guilty on most of the charges; later that year, the other charges were dropped for lack of evidence. The verdicts resulted from the investigation of two critical elements in the case: the way the children were questioned and the validity of their answers. The children had originally been questioned by people who already believed that a Satanic cult was at work in the preschool, and the questions and methods the examiners used encouraged the children to say what the examiners wanted them to say to build their case. As a result, much of the children's testimony was so tainted that it could not be presented in court. Because most of the charges were based on the children's accusations, the prosecutors then had little with which to charge the Buckeys.

However, even if the children's accusations could not have been used in court, their stories could have pointed prosecutors to supporting evidence. But the tales the children told just did not check out. Authorities dug under the school to find the secret room; they found none. Then authorities dug up the backyard, looking for bones of sacrificial victims; they came up empty-handed this time, too. And some of the children who were the most vocal in attacking Ray Buckey had attended the school before Buckey had worked there.

Shortly after the McMartin case made headlines, other accusations of Satanic cult abuse of children received national attention. In September 1983, only one month after the McMartin case became public, twenty-four adults in Jordan, Minnesota, were accused of murdering and mutilating children. The following month, children in foster care in Nebraska accused their parents in Arizona of being part of a cult that kidnapped children from shopping malls and then sacrificed them to the Devil. Similar charges were brought forth the following spring in Nevada, Tennessee, and Illinois, where more than two hundred allegations were made against a single group of preschool teachers. By the fall of 1984, teachers in sixty-three day-care centers in Southern California alone were under investigation. Within the following two years, day-care centers in Oregon, Texas, Nevada, and Washington State were charged with Satanic sexual abuse.[9] Many critics compared the search for Satanists to the Salem witch hunt. No proof was ever found of any Satanic cult abuse. When accusers failed to win in court, accusations suddenly stopped.

The Church of Satan

The only group of Satanists who have publicly promoted their beliefs are members of the Church of Satan, which was started by Anton LaVey in 1966. Because LaVey could find little about Satanism to guide him in forming this new cult, he developed his own set of beliefs and rituals. He published *The Satanic Bible* in 1969 and *The Satanic Rituals* in 1972.

LaVey told followers to do whatever they wanted to as long as it did not hurt others unnecessarily. While most religions held that human beings were by nature sinful and therefore had to be taught restraint and concern for their neighbors, LaVey urged followers to do what came naturally. For instance, instead of turning the other cheek when someone had wronged you, LaVey advocated taking vengeance. He also thought that being kind to everyone was a waste; members should only be kind to those who deserved it. He urged his followers to celebrate this life to the fullest, taking pleasure and rewards now, not waiting for a heaven that might never come.

The Church of Satan has probably never had more than one thousand members, even though LaVey estimated that he at one time had twenty-five thousand followers. His church was greatly weakened when, in 1975, two followers, Michael Aquino and Lilith Sinclair, broke away and started a new Satanic cult, the Temple of Set, named after an ancient Egyptian deity named Set, believed to be the figure upon which the Christian version of the Devil is based. Today, the Church of Satan holds public worship services and encourages new members to join. However, it is unlikely that many Americans will convert to Satanism—the public's loathing of the Devil is simply too strong.

10

Results of Cults

Clearly, cults that have made headlines have angered and even terrified Americans. As a result, opposition to all cults has been strong. Even so, most citizens have done little beyond pointing out a cult's supposed faults.

Some Americans, however, have become deeply opposed to a cult's practices, especially if the cult is in their neighborhood, and they have taken action to curb these practices. Citizens opposed to the Santería cult in Hialeah, Florida, are a good example of people trying to control a cult's actions on a local level. Opponents led a petition drive and persuaded the city's officials to enact ordinances that would eliminate the cult's ability to sacrifice animals—although these ordinances were later declared unconstitutional.

In some cases, local opponents have encouraged law officials to study a cult and its actions carefully, looking for violations that might lead to the arrest of the cult's leader or leaders and perhaps result in the demise of the cult. Opponents of Rajneesh's cult in Oregon, for instance, after diligent search, found out that immigration laws had been violated. Other cults have lost their leaders after they have been convicted of income tax evasion or weapons violations.

Anticult Organizations

Although many citizens concerned about cults have been active only on a local level, others have banded together and started national anticult organizations. Some of these groups were started and funded by conservative Christians who considered any non-Christian group a cult. The best known of these organizations—the Spiritual Counterfeits Project, the Christian Research Institute, and the InterVarsity Christian Fellowship—all are active today and limit their activities to informing the public about the beliefs held by cults.

A second group of anticultists, secular opponents, are concerned about cult lifestyles and practices. These groups were started in the 1970s by parents whose children had joined cults. One of the first groups to organize consisted of parents whose sons and daughters had joined the Children of God. Members of this group, known as FREECOG (Free Our Children from the Children of God), were determined to get their sons and daughters out of the cult.

When distraught parents whose offspring had joined other cults heard about FREECOG, they sought the organization's aid. FREECOG then changed its focus to include all parents who wanted help because their children

111

had joined cults. The organization also changed its name to Volunteer Parents of America (VPA). Later, VPA, joined by other volunteer groups, became the Citizen's Freedom Foundation. The organization is known today as the Cult Awareness Network (CAN).

None of these groups has had more than two thousand active members at any one time. However, they were very determined members, some of whom had suffered immeasurably because of tragedies involving cults. One of the leaders of CAN, for example, was Patricia Ryan, whose father, United States Representative Leo J. Ryan, was killed by members of the People's Temple in Jonestown, Guyana. The groups developed a four-point program to curb cults and their influence: education, deprogramming, lawsuits, and legislation.

Education

The secular anticult groups have had their greatest success with their education programs. They have established a frightening image of cults that, in general, has been accepted by the American public. In addition, they have published books and pamphlets about the dangers of cults, which encourage readers to think seriously about the group they want to join. Members of these secular groups have often appeared on news programs to discuss cults from their viewpoint.

Cults have not been happy with the way they have been described by anticult groups, and some have fought back with great vigor. Scientologists, for example, have started an education program of their own, openly using information to discredit their opponents, especially the leaders of CAN.

Scientologists also have publicly called the Cult Awareness Network a "hate group," and they have charged it with "religious discrimination, spreading false propaganda, and promoting abuses of minority religions."[1] In addition, Scientologists were in the forefront pointing out the role that anticultists played in the Waco tragedy by portraying the Davidians as dangerous and encouraging federal agents to use force to arrest David Koresh.[2]

Deprogramming

The second point of the secular anticultists' four-point program was—and still is—deprogramming. One of the founders of FREECOG, Ted Patrick, was among the first to deprogram cultists. Alarmed after his son had been approached and greatly affected by recruiters representing the Children of God, Patrick had quit his job as a California state employee in the early 1970s and had become, instead, a self-appointed warrior for the anticult movement. Patrick believed that cults first hypnotized would-be members and then brainwashed them into staying. All of this was done, he thought, as part of a Communist plot to take over America by destroying its citizens' ability to think. Patrick set out to stop this from happening by making it possible for cultists to reason again—at a cost of ten thousand dollars or more per member.

Patrick's program involved three steps once his services were requested, usually by parents of a child in a cult. Unless the subject could be lured away from the cult under false pretenses such as a family illness, Patrick literally kidnapped the member, using as many men and as much force as necessary to drag the victim away and then take him or her to a secluded place. Here the member was often verbally assaulted until he or she renounced the cult. In effect, Patrick used the same techniques that he accused cults of using: isolation, indoctrination, and, finally, trying to force the victim to accept a different set of beliefs.

Patrick, and the others who joined him in the deprogramming business, claimed to have great success. Still, when parents who had hired deprogrammers were questioned about the results of their efforts by the editor of *The Advisor*, a newsletter concerned with cult issues, almost half of them admitted that the deprogramming had failed. In several cases, parents had to have their children deprogrammed two and even three times before they were willing to renounce their cult.[3]

Cults Fight Deprogrammers

Even though deprogramming was not a total success, cults were scared of it. To protect cult members, leaders taught their followers how to resist by pretending to go along with the deprogrammers until they found a way to escape or by praying aloud in order to drown out the verbal assaults. Cults also filed charges against deprogrammers in order to put an end to the attacks.

Once the cases reached the courts and were covered by the media, Americans became outraged by the deprogrammers' assaults. Conservative Christian groups, who had long been dismayed by the beliefs that cults expressed, were among the most vocal in speaking out about the methods being used by Patrick and the others.

One Christian leader, Walter Martin, spoke for many when he said, "I cannot stand behind such practices. It is true that cultists have been blinded . . . but it is also true that they have the right to make up their own minds, and we should not stoop to unChristian tactics to accomplish God's ends."[4]

The courts were not in favor of forceful deprogramming either. Judges ordered hefty fines and even jail time for those who had participated in such actions, treating the kidnappings as a violent crime.

Over the years, the courts' opposition, mounting legal costs, and unfavorable publicity seemed to have put an end to deprogramming. Then, in May 1992, Debra Dobkowski was abducted on a street in Washington, D.C. Three men, led by deprogrammer Galen Kelly, grabbed Dobkowski as she was walking to her car. They knocked her to the ground and dragged her by her ankles to a waiting van. Then they rushed her to the deprogramming site, where the woman who had hired them was waiting. The men were aghast when the woman, who was the mother of Dobkowski's roommate, Beth Bruckert, told them that they had brought the wrong person. Her daughter, Beth, was the target, not Debra Dobkowski.

Understandably, Dobkowski was very upset and very angry, and she filed charges. Kelly eventually pleaded guilty to misprison, which is a felony.

Another case of deprogramming also drew attention to the continuing practice. In October 1995, Jason Scott, who had been forcibly deprogrammed in 1991, was awarded $4.8 million in compensation. Rick Ross, the accused deprogrammer, was ordered to pay $3.8 million, and CAN, which was accused of recommending Ross's services, was ordered to pay one million dollars. CAN has announced that it will appeal the decision. Whether or not these cases will be the last deprogramming charges to reach court is not certain.

Lawsuits Galore

The third point of the anticultists' program was to curb cults with the help of the courts using several different approaches. First, parents whose children were in cults asked the courts for special powers, conservatorships, that would enable them to legally make decisions for their children, including having them deprogrammed, even if the children were adults. In general, courts, which usually give conservatorships to children of elderly and incapacitated parents, refused to grant such power to parents.

Second, anticultists, parents, and former cult members who had turned upon their cult sued for financial compensation for the harm the cult had supposedly done. Although several former members did receive large sums, many lost their cases. This was due, in part, to the fact that courts did not accept the brainwashing or mind control arguments put forth by the anticultists. Instead, the courts usually took the position that cult members had willingly become members of the organizations, which made it much more difficult for former members and their parents to win.

Cults also filed lawsuits. This was especially true of the Scientologists. They have filed more than forty-five lawsuits against CAN between 1991 and 1993 as well as dozens of human-rights complaints. Only one of these lawsuits has been won by the cult.

Because so many suits were filed by Scientologists, CAN accused the cult of harassment. CAN then filed a lawsuit of its own, accusing the Scientologists of trying to destroy the Network by driving it into bankruptcy through numerous and expensive lawsuits. In fact, CAN was forced to file for bankruptcy in October 1995.

More Court Cases

In addition to suing their critics, cults have fought attempts to curb them by going to court to defend their right to worship as they please. For example, Jehovah's Witnesses have fought laws that said that they had to salute the flag as well as laws that limited their right to hand out religious literature or speak to groups about their beliefs.

In all cases, the courts have upheld the right of cult members to believe whatever they wish—and in effect, these cults have reinforced the cherished right of religious freedom for all Americans. At the same time, the courts have taken into account the dangers presented by some of these beliefs and placed some restrictions on *practices*—handling poisonous snakes, for example, or refusing medical attention for children—that might endanger lives. This stance attempts to ensure religious freedom and protect members of cults as well as society in general.

Legislation

Even though the courts have tried to protect both society and cult members, history teaches us that more tragedies are likely to occur. As a result, critics of cults continue to argue that cults should somehow be controlled.

Anticultists agree, and they have, as the fourth point of their program, sought assistance from state legislators to restrain cults. One of the earliest instances was in California in 1974, when parents convinced State Senator Mervyn M. Dymally to hold hearings on cults and their impact on children. More recently, after the deaths of the Branch Davidians, similar hearings were held in Illinois. To date, many hearings have been scheduled, but none has resulted in new anticult legislation.

Even so, cult members decry these hearings. Using the anticultists' estimate that there are five thousand cults in the United States, members point out that only a very few of them have ever made headlines or been convicted of a crime. And, members are quick to add, if cult members or leaders break the law, they can be punished, just as any other American would be. Legislation to curb cults, they insist, is unnecessary, unfair, and unconstitutional.

Lowell Streiker, who began a counseling service for former cult members after the Jonestown tragedy, supported the cults' arguments about violence when he wrote:

> Every year, a few members of cults or sects commit suicide and a handful of fanatics act out their paranoid delusions to the bitter end—dying in a shoot-out with police or murdering an innocent victim or causing a death through negligence. Such behavior is intolerable. But, in all fairness, I must point out that the suicide rate among my clients . . . who are involved in cults and the rate of their involvement in violent crime or self-destructive acts are negligible compared to the incidence of such things in the general population. America is the most

118

violent industrialized nation on the face of the earth. Our prisons are filled to overflowing. An incredibly high percentage of our children will be . . . abused before they reach adulthood. . . . Yes, fanatic groups are frustrating and threatening on a case-by-case basis. . . . But let us not lose perspective.[5]

Still, the images of Jonestown and Waco haunt Americans.

More Results

Besides raising tempers and giving Americans lots of ideas to consider, cults have had some other interesting effects on American society. Sites of some of the oldest cults, such as the Shaker villages, have become popular places for tourists to visit—a fact that would surely surprise the first Shakers.

The Amana Colonies in Iowa, site of a cult that lasted almost one hundred years, is now one of Iowa's top tourist attractions, where visitors seek out the woolen products for which the colonies have long been famous, devour food prepared as it was when the commune was in full swing, and attend historic presentations in the colonies' schoolhouse to get a feel for what the members' lives were like.

Americans also regularly visit historic sites associated with other cults. Visitors tour the Mormons' early settlement in Nauvoo, Illinois, as well as the church's world-famous Tabernacle in Salt Lake City, Utah. One of the biggest tourist attractions in West Virginia is the Hare Krishna settlement in New Vrindaban, whose members were once threatened by thugs.

Although foretelling the future was forbidden in Salem, Massachusetts, when the Puritans were in charge, attempts to do so nowadays are commonplace and often done in fun. Spiritualists used a variety of methods to contact the other world, including a Ouija® board, which is now sold in most American toy stores. Many of the people involved with the New Age movement used the ancient fortune-telling devices of tarot cards or the position of the stars to predict the future. Almost every major newspaper now carries horoscopes, and tarot cards are readily available. And anyone trying to influence the future by carrying a lucky rabbit's foot or hanging a horseshoe above the door is using charms long associated with Voodoo.

Spiritualists and New Agers popularized meditation and yoga, both of which were viewed as ways to reach greater self-awareness and self-fulfillment. Meditation and yoga soon spread from cults into society in general, and were readily adopted as methods of gaining power over one's life as well as a way of reducing stress.

The Theosophists had a great effect on Montessori schools, which have long been popular in America. Maria Montessori, the Italian woman who founded the schools, studied with the Theosophists in India for nine years, because, like the cult's leaders, she was seeking new ways to improve human nature. She was deeply influenced by Madame Blavatsky's emphasis on using all of one's senses to experience one's surroundings in order to learn. Smelling a rose and touching its petals were as important to learning, in both women's opinion, as reading about roses or being told about them. Children in Montessori

Cults have had many effects on American society. Some communes are now popular historic sites that produce highly sought after handmade items. Cults have also affected modern art, games, the popularity of fortune-telling, and even the use of good luck charms.

schools are encouraged to explore their world, not just read about it.

Finally, one of the oldest religious cults, the secret cult of Mithras, which flourished in ancient Rome, established a holiday on what cult followers believed was the shortest day of the year, December 25. They held the celebration to rejoice in the return of the sun, the symbol of Mithras. The first Christians, uncertain about the exact date of Christ's birth, decided to celebrate his birthday at the same time, establishing once and for all Christmas Day—one of America's most highly celebrated holidays.

In Conclusion

Now that you know more about cults, do you think that they have been a negative or a positive force on American society? Is the American public well informed about cults? Should cults be studied as a subject in school? And, most important, what role should cults play in America's future?

Chapter Notes

Chapter 1

1. Nancy Gibbs, "Tragedy in Waco," *Time*, May 3, 1993, p. 41.
2. Ibid., p. 42.
3. Ginia Bellafante, "Waco: The Flame Still Burns," *Time*, May 1, 1995, p. 47.
4. Ibid.

Chapter 2

1. Margaret Thaler Singer with Janja Lalich, *Cults in Our Midst* (San Francisco: Jossey-Bass Publishers, 1995), p. 5.
2. J. Gordon Melton, *Encyclopedic Handbook of Cults in America* (New York: Garland Publishing, 1992), pp. 7–8.
3. Willa Appel, *Cults in America: Programmed for Paradise* (New York: Holt, Rinehart & Winston, 1983), p. 54.
4. Ibid., pp. 59–60.
5. Ibid., p. 61.

Chapter 3

1. Nat Hentoff, *Free Speech for Me—But Not for Thee* (New York: HarperCollins, 1992), p. 243.
2. Vincent Bugliosi with Curt Gentry, *Helter Skelter: The True Story of the Manson Murders* (New York: W. W. Norton & Co., 1994), p. 233.

Chapter 4

1. George Klineman, Sherman Butler, and David Conn, *The Cult That Died: The Tragedy of Jim Jones and the People's Temple* (New York: G. P. Putnam's Sons, 1980), pp. 358–359.
2. Ibid., p. 364.
3. Keith Harrary, "The Truth About Jonestown," in Robert Emmet Long, ed., *Religious Cults in America* (New York: H. W. Wilson Co., 1994), p. 17.

Chapter 5

1. Edward Rice, *American Saints & Seers: American-Born Religions & the Genius Behind Them* (New York: Four Winds Press, 1982), p. 149.

2. J. Gordon Melton, *Encyclopedic Handbook of Cults in America* (New York: Garland Publishing, 1992), p. 126.

3. Margaret Thaler Singer with Janja Lalich, *Cults in Our Midst* (San Francisco: Jossey-Bass Publishers, 1995), p. 43.

Chapter 6

1. Willa Appel, *Cults in America: Programmed for Paradise* (New York: Holt, Rinehart & Winston, 1983), p. 62.

2. Ibid., p. 79.

3. J. Gordon Melton, *Encyclopedic Handbook of Cults in America* (New York: Garland Publishing, 1992), p. 226.

4. Eileen Barker, *The Making of a Moonie: Choice or Brainwashing?* (New York: Basil Blackwell, 1984), p. 222.

5. James D. Tabor and Eugene V. Gallagher, *Why Waco?: Cults and the Battle for Religious Freedom in America* (Berkeley, Calif.: University of California Press, 1995), p. 157.

Chapter 7

1. J. Gordon Melton, *Encyclopedic Handbook of Cults in America* (New York: Garland Publishing, 1992), pp. 239–240.

2. Ibid., pp. 245–247.

3. Rachel Storm, *In Search of Heaven on Earth* (London, England: Bloomsbury, 1991), p. 175.

4. Mark Whitaker, "And Now What?" *Newsweek*, October 30, 1995, p. 30.

Chapter 8

1. Carol F. Karlsen, *The Devil in the Shape of a Woman: Witchcraft in Colonial New England* (New York: W. W. Norton & Co., 1987), p. xii.

2. Margot Adler, *Drawing Down the Moon: Witches, Druids, Goddess-Worshippers, and Other Pagans in America Today* (New York: Viking Press, 1979), p. 151.

3. J. Gordon Melton, *Encyclopedic Handbook of Cults in America* (New York: Garland Publishing, 1992), p. 368.

4. Bob Cohn and David A. Kaplan, "A Chicken on Every Altar?" in Robert Emmet Long, ed., *Religious Cults in America* (New York: H.W. Wilson Co., 1994), p. 149.

Chapter 9

1. Jeffrey S. Victor, *Satanic Panic: The Creation of a Contemporary Legend* (Chicago: Open Court, 1993), p. 203.

2. Nancy Garden, *Devils and Demons* (Philadelphia: J. B. Lippincott Co., 1976), p. 127.

3. Victor, p. 346.

4. Ibid., pp. 334–354.

5. Ibid., p. 81.

6. Ibid., p. 100.

7. Ibid., p. 80.

8. Robert D. Hicks, *In Pursuit of Satan: The Police and the Occult* (Buffalo, N.Y.: Prometheus Books, 1991), pp. 187–188.

9. Victor, pp. 355–361.

Chapter 10

1. Joe Maxwell, "Cult-Watchers File Lawsuit," *Christianity Today*, April 4, 1994, p. 84.

2. Alexander Cockburn, "Beat the Devil: Waco Revisited," *The Nation*, October 18, 1993, p. 414.

3. Willa Appel, *Cults in America: Programmed for Paradise* (New York: Holt, Rinehart & Winston, 1983), pp. 148–149.

4. J. Gordon Melton, *Encyclopedic Handbook of Cults in America* (New York: Garland Publishing, 1992), p. 349.

5. Lowell D. Streiker, *Mind-Bending: Brainwashing, Cults, and Deprogramming in the '80s* (Garden City, N.Y.: Doubleday & Co., 1984), pp. 200–201.

Further Reading

Bach, Marcus. *Strange Sects and Curious Cults.* New York: Dodd, Mead & Company, 1961.

Nardo, Don, and Erik Belgum. *Voodoo: Opposing Viewpoints.* San Diego, Calif.: Greenhaven Press, 1991.

Rice, Edward. *American Saints & Seers: American-Born Religions & the Genius Behind Them.* New York: Four Winds Press, 1982.

Streissguth, Thomas. *Charismatic Cult Leaders.* Minneapolis, Minn.: Oliver Press, 1995.

Zeinert, Karen. *The Salem Witchcraft Trials.* New York: Franklin Watts, 1989.

Index